Humble The Poet

UNLEARN

101 Simple Truths
for a Better Life

This Project was completed with the very generous support and contributions of the following:

Brwnppl.com
Karim Lakhani
Nadia Asimi
Darshan Dorka
B-Coalition
Amanpreet Sidhu
SUPPORT ALL SOIL
Satish Kanwar
Davinder Toor
Rick & Harjot Matharu
Pavinder & Karmjit Athwal
Harwinder Mander
Aiksimar Singh
Jagmeet Singh MPP
Itvinder Singh
Gurdev Singh & Balbir Kaur Mahl (My Parents)

CONTENTS

"To attain knowledge,
add things everyday.
To attain wisdom, remove
things every day."

- Lao Tzu

0

WHY?

The journey of my life is no different than the journey of any one else on this planet. There have been brilliant moments and moments that still make me cringe when I think about them. I'm haunted by my past, and worried about my future just as much as anyone else. I'm confident that I'm not the only one going through the peaks and valleys of life. The realization that I'm not alone allows me to understand how normal these things really are. We tend to amplify our problems and sink into a centre-of-the-world mentality, thinking that the entire universe is conspiring against us; it's not.

We all have conversations with ourselves; in the shower, on the way to work, late at night –sleepless in bed. I took these conversations, and just started typing and sharing them with the people in my life who wanted to hear them. If you're reading this, that includes you.

Loneliness can be a horrid feeling, and it's amazing how quickly it can dissipate when we realize how much we have in common with others folks; ironically the room is full of folks who feel alone. The remedy I found that best works to combat this feeling is to simply connect with others.

I'm an observer and a creator. This means I simply try to pay attention and restate what I've learned in the way I understood it. I worked as an elementary school teacher for over half a decade, and those experiences taught me to keep my communications short and sweet. Information in small chunks is easier to absorb. That's what this book is, a collection of nuggets to remind you of the things that keep this wild ride steady. I use the word remind because we have all had our flashes of brilliance and greatness throughout life, and whether or not we knew it, the mindsets we had during those moments can be applied to our challenges today, to help us overcome them.

I appreciate the time you've taken to check this out and hope you enjoy my work as much as I enjoyed writing it. Please soak in what you like, disregard what you don't, and share whatever you feel someone else needs to hear.

One Luv

Kanwer Singh
'Humble The Poet'

1

NO STRAIGHT LINES

There aren't very many straight lines in nature, and that includes your life. When reading through this book, the first thing I want you to let go of is the idea of a straight line. You're going to come to points in this book where you stop and say, "Didn't he already say that?" The answer is, "YES!" Anything worth saying is worth repeating. It's rare that we come across something worthwhile in life, and a single encounter is enough for it to stay with us. This book was written as much more of a cycle than simply having a beginning, middle and end.

Ideas need to be reinforced and revisited to settle themselves into us. These days, information is being taken in at such a rate that it's forgotten before the page is even turned (assuming people still turn pages). Any skill worth having requires practice, and practice is simply repetition over and over until it becomes second nature.

There's very little order in this book; you can read it backwards, start from the middle, or read every other chapter; the content here only has value when it connects with you. What you read at 15 will have a completely different relevance when you're 25. I hope you decide to revisit these writings and build new connections with the ideas as your own journey continues.

The thoughts and ideas presented are nothing revolutionary. They've been around for thousands of years, and most of this wisdom already exists within us, we just need to shed some of the other things the world has put on top. We gain more from letting go, there's nothing mystical and secretive about this idea. This book is meant to agree with, and bring out the wisdom you already possess.

No matter the shape of your life and journey, I hope this book makes the trip a bit more enjoyable.

We gain more from letting go,
there's nothing mystical and
secretive about this idea.

2 **WANT TO BE HAPPIER IN 5 EASY STEPS?**

Just send 19.99 to... I'm kidding.

Write down five things in your life that you're grateful for, or write ten.

A simple shift in what your mind is paying attention to can do wonders for the way you feel. It's not a trick, it's not a gimmick, it's respecting the fact that happiness is a mindset, so SET YOUR MIND TO HAPPINESS BY THINKING OF HAPPY SH*T.

It doesn't last, but is it supposed to? Does it make sense to be happy ALL the time? If you were happy all the time, would we even know what happiness was anymore?

Improve your relationship with all your emotions because there's a lot to discover from them. I'm grateful that I have a variety of emotions. They teach me something new about myself on a regular basis.

We hide the darkness with our smiles, feel lonely in crowded rooms, and become so accustomed to these feelings that we begin to believe they're apart of who we are.

They're not. You won't be the same person if you let them go, you'll be better.

People who aren't happy with what they have won't be happy with what they get. This mindset can be both beneficial and burdensome. Some folks find happiness in the pursuit itself and are grateful for the opportunity.

Personally, I'm not looking to be happy all the time nor do I want to be satisfied and content. I enjoy an ambitious hunger, and as long as I'm moving forward, learning, sharing, and growing, I'll be grateful for every nugget that comes my way, whether it be sh*t or gold.

What are you grateful for?

We hide the darkness with our smiles, feel lonely in crowded rooms, and become so accustomed to these feelings that we begin to believe they're a part of who we are.

3 UNHAPPINESS IS SIMPLE

Unhappiness is simply when the picture in your head doesn't match the picture in front of you. Some folks aren't happy because they don't have what they want, or they aren't where they wish to be. Some just feel horrible about themselves. Maybe they're comparing themselves to others, or even a former version of themselves. Either way, the simple equation is the mismatch of how you want it with how it is.

How you want it isn't set in stone. Most of us have wanted something for a long time, and once receiving it, realize it wasn't all that, and what we had propped up in our mind was an inflated sense of euphoria or contentment. Wanting less will definitely make you happier than getting more.

How it is isn't set in stone either. We see what we choose. Most of the improvements I've made in my life this past year came from tweaking the way I saw the things that were always around me. I stopped seeing my mistakes as failures, but rather valuable (or expensive) lessons. Roadblocks became speed bumps and hurdles. Reasons to quit became reasons to adapt (or motivation to smash through).

Let's not get it twisted, I'm not a Zen Buddha baby. Bellyaching is still an art to me and I complain about things that make first world problems look legit. I do, however, only give myself about 10 minutes to be a Sad Panda before I move forward. I ask myself, "How did you want it," re-evaluate how it is, and try to tweak and adjust both to bring them a bit closer together.

Expectations are a bigger enemy to our happiness than our

16

circumstances; the less expectations you have, the better off you are. Couple that with a Positive Pete set of goggles, and things will feel even a bit more smile-worthy.

It's also important to remember that everlasting happiness is a concept only promised by preachers and infomercials. It's healthy to have a myriad (that's a smart word for "a bunch") of emotions occupying the hotel of your heart. Welcome them all in, and experience them the way they're meant to be (just clean up afterwards). You'll also realize the relationships between them. The less things anger you, the less things will excite you. The less things make you cry, the less things will make you laugh. Different life experiences are going to break barriers within you and you'll respond emotionally to things you never connected to before (like getting all teary eyed every time you watch the end of that Fresh Prince episode when his pops bails on him *sniff*)

The next time you're having a Sad Panda moment can be the next time you ask yourself about the picture in your head, and the picture in front of you. That moment of realization and discovery will put you in a position of power to mold both ends to bring them closer together. It works better than junk food, sometimes that is.

PLEASE NOTE: Emotions are related to chemicals in your brain and a few paragraphs from a rhyming Beardo may not suffice. Don't ever be afraid to seek help if you start to feel helpless and overwhelmed. I have, and it has helped a lot.

Expectations are a bigger enemy to our happiness than our circumstances.

4 THE GIFT OF FEAR

Fear is a gift.

I'm talking about the fear we have as creatures that gives us a jolt when in danger. The jolt either gives us what's necessary to deal with that danger, or what's necessary to get the f*ck out of the way. That type of fear is something we only feel in the present and generally lasts for a short time.

Humans are funny creatures because we can carry fears even when out of danger. If you've ever been a victim of crime you know how it lingers and disrupts the normalcy of your life for quite some time. It messes with your sleep, keeps you on edge in seemingly safe situations, and can serve to paralyze you when you try to move forward.

On top of that, we have this awesome (remembering that the word awesome doesn't always mean a good thing) ability to create fear, not only in ourselves, but also in others. These fears include (but aren't limited to) fear of failure, fear of disappointment, fear of embarrassment, fear of loss, fear of change, and fear of truth. These fears are technically considered phobias because they're irrational, and don't actually involve danger.

Asking that girl for her number and having her reply with an "eww no" isn't going to be the end of your existence. It may feel sh*tty, and the desire to not feel sh*tty may keep you from asking her. The same way the fear of disappointing others keeps you from switching out of Biology class into a Modern Dance class; dating outside your bubble; or leaving your job as a teacher to be a rap singer.

These phobia type fears aren't gifts like the adrenaline rush you get when the car in front of you stops suddenly, and you need to react tout suite. That adrenaline goes away after a few minutes since it has served its purpose. Phobias only seem to grow in magnitude and multiply.

We all have these phobias, and the ones we carry are as unique as we are. As a mass of people, we can have collective phobias, and these phobias have been exploited and used to control us like lab rats for decades (word to Edward Bernays).

We avoid those feelings by playing it safe, or playing along. Our fear of exclusion motivates our assimilation. Our fear of not being noticed motivates our loud behavior. Our fear of loneliness motivates the personal sacrifices and compromises we think are necessary to be accepted by others. We're all doing the same dance, but think we're in it alone because we're moving to different music.

The courage we need to develop is not the 'knight in shining armor super duper confidence unfazed' courage. It's the recognition of what we fear, and deciding that even with the tiniest baby steps, we move forward despite them. What you fear isn't the roadblock; allowing the fear to keep you from moving is the real obstacle. FDR said it during one of America's lowest times, "The only thing to fear is fear itself."

Whenever I have issues or find myself feeling uneasy or hesitant, I ask myself, "What are you afraid of?" Answering that question clarifies who I am, and it's the first step to overcoming that fear. In most cases, what I fear is dramatically worse than the reality of the situation.

As I go through these adventures being a public figure and hear every opinion across the spectrum, everything I ever feared people would think of me, they already have. Yet here I am, still breathing, beard still soft, rhymes only getting better, learning lessons even quicker. I've seen people dig themselves out of holes a million times worse than some of my created phobias.

No one is fearless, but the bravest people I know are those most in tune with their fears and phobias, and have decided not to let those get in the way of their happiness.

As always, this is going to require you to have a conversation with yourself to discover these fears. Identifying them will be the first step to conquering them.

The bravest people I know are those most in tune with their fears and phobias, and have decided not to let those get in the way of their happiness.

5 GOLDEN GIRLS

In the thickest New York accent you can imagine, one old lady says to another, "Let's have strawberry shortcake to celebrate another day on Earth." When the cake arrives the lady asks the waitress, "Did you remember to take out the calories?"

It was a Golden Girls moment (word to Sikh Knowledge), and it also reminded me of the never-ending power we have to paint the world we want to see.

There's a lot of bullsh*t in the world. I've spent the majority of my artistic existence trying to shine a light on that bullsh*t. A result of doing so, required me to dig deeper into issues, and myself, if I ever wanted to have anything new to say, without sounding like a (complete) hypocrite, with opinions on issues we all contribute to. I learned a lot about how truth has no place in a world where people only want to see two sides: their side and the other side. The world is ten shades of grey, but that's not very convenient for those who want to see in black and white, since that's how they choose to paint the picture.

As humans, we seek affirmation over information. In simpler terms, we look for evidence to support what we already believe, and subconsciously ignore the things that contradict that. This isn't necessarily a bad thing. If we didn't have a device in our brains to ignore what we thought irrelevant, we'd be overloaded with redunkoulous amounts of information that comes at us every second of the day.

This can be a bit damaging if you're married to an idea, and the repetition of information and people that validate that idea are all things you choose to expose yourself to (those are the key ingredients to your comfort zone). On top of that, it can be dramatically worse if the view you have on the world, is that it is nothing but sh*t. Simply put, if you think life sucks, life will suck; and you'll ignore your full fridge, running water, access to internet, and ability to have leisure time to even contemplate how much life sucks.

Do you focus on the people that love you, or the ones that won't return your calls? Do you share your problems or your joys with people? Realize, every thought you have is a brushstroke on the world you see. None of this negates the extreme issues the world is facing, but let's not lose sight that many, if not most, of these issues were always in existence. Even viewing these issues is an opportunity for you to find some additional gratitude in the life you have, and motivation to spread some beauty, even if it's on a local level.

The only reason you're not good enough is because you're thinking it. When I went to the Tim Burton exhibition, the first thing they showed was a rejection letter he received early in his career. He didn't let that circumstance change the picture he was painting.

The old lady came up with the idea of ordering the strawberry shortcake after hearing another table sing happy birthday for their friend. She found inspiration in their celebration and found an excuse to celebrate herself.

Make an excuse to be happy right now and start painting with those thoughts. Your life is art, a work in progress at that, and it's only complete when you're dead. Everyday is a new day to see it the way you want.

Realize, every thought
you have is a brushstroke
on the world you see

6 DEATHTRAP FOR DEPENDENCIES

Relationships can be a deathtrap for dependencies.

I'm not talking solely about romantic relationships, I'm talking the whole shebang: professional, friends, creative, family, etc.

I'm not anti-relationship, I'm just pro-watch-out-for-developing-dependencies-in-your-relationship. When we put the key to our happiness in the pocket of others, we're now at their mercy. Not all folks are looking to exploit the power they've been granted, but sh*t still tends to happen.

The most important relationship you have is with yourself, simple. Putting the responsibility of your smiles on anyone else will often lead to the opposite, and you have no one else to blame except yourself. This anti-victim mentality isn't popular because people don't enjoy the onus, but it's probably the only way to ensure a longstanding healthy ability to have meaningful relationships.

We've cheapened the word *love* to the point that it's common for someone to say they love you, and then no longer mean it a short time later. What is love really? Does a mother fall out of love with her child? If the dynamics of any relationship changes, what usually causes it?

One of the answers is expectation. The love we seek is generally riddled in conditions, but the fairy tales make us feel that it's unconditional. Respecting the fact that relationships are based on conditions may not be the most romantic, but it is the most realistic.

I encourage you to be independent, not because I want you to be, but because you already are. We're born alone and die alone, and again, though that lacks romance, ensuring you put your relationship with yourself first, dramatically enhances your ability to have relationships with others.

Dependencies aren't healthy, whether it is to a substance, idea, or another human being. In this sense, wanting less results in having more. Again, I'm not an idealist. In our daily lives we have to depend on people for things to get done, but if we acknowledge the dependencies early, it cushions the blow dramatically if expectations aren't met. It can also serve to motivate us to be in a position to further reduce the dependencies we can survive without.

I'm not advocating a life of complete isolation and simplicity. I've always had a life rich with people and complexity, but at the same time, I do find peace in simplifying and cleaning the clutter.

I also know if you're not happy with yourself, nothing can compensate to fill that void.

The most important
relationship you have is
with yourself, simple.

7

WE CARRY A LOT THROUGH OUR LIVES

I know everyone reading this is haunted by a memory of regret. Some bone-headed moment that you'd pay your left arm to get back; a mistake, which in hindsight, seemed so easy to spot, but not at the time.

Some of us will spend our days daydreaming of what life would have been like, had we not made that mistake; oh, how much better everything would be.
Snap out of that sh*t.

You can't predict the future, not even in your imaginary 'what if' scenarios. When we're not happy with our present, we can start wishing away our future, by focusing on the past, or... we can do something about it NOW.

Regret is a burden we all hold, for whatever reason, and holding on does nothing but weigh us down. Learn from the mistakes of your past, thank them for occurring, and then gently push them into the wind, and wave as they flutter away.

No decision is ever absolutely great, or absolutely horrible, stop thinking so extreme. Understand your past, don't waste time judging it. Understand your present, don't waste time judging it. Use what you learn from these understandings to help create the future you want. This isn't easy, and I promise you'll f*ck up some more in the future, but be ready for that, and once it happens, start digging for the jewels of wisdom that come from those foibles.

Folks can only love you for yesterday, but you can appreciate yourself for your present. Take a super deep breath, and hold it. Hold it a bit longer, then slowly breathe it out, and keep blowing until there's no air in your lungs. Congratulations, you just pressed reset.

Now move forward and create a life you want.

Regret is a burden we all hold,
for whatever reason, and
holding does nothing
but weigh us down.

8 WHEN LESS IS MORE

The less you give a damn, the happier you'll be. Create a life that feels good on the inside, not one that simply looks good from the outside.

We can't see other peoples' struggles, pains, pressures, and anxieties. We see the same front they put up that we do. Trying to evaluate your life in comparison to others will always leave you more depressed for that simple reason.

When we focus on creating happiness from the outside then in, we'll continue to fail because we're using other people's measures of success, and pretending they're our own. What makes you feel like a million bucks may involve a pair of ripped jeans and that t-shirt with the holes in it. How you feel is more important than how you look, and though I agree staying fresh can help the way you feel, the best you thing you can wear is your confidence and happiness.

Don't care what others think until you've taken your own thoughts into consideration. You can't predict what other people think, and even if you could, it's impossible to make everyone happy. The world is full of diverse opinions, and some of those opinions are in your favour, and some are not.

I don't have the ability to get to know all of you on a personal level, but I'm super confident there's something unique about all of you worth bringing to the forefront. Make your happiness worth more than the opinions of others.

Give a damn about yourself first, then those who give a damn about you, and then see if you have any damns left to give.

Give a damn about yourself
first, then those who give
a damn about you, and
then see if you have any
damns left to give.

9 LOVING A BOTTOMLESS PIT

Loving someone can sometimes feel like you're pouring everything into a bottomless pit.

You would give anything just to hear a splash at the end, just to feel they're aware of your efforts and energy because right now, nothing feels good enough.

Maybe you can try harder, maybe you're not doing enough, maybe you're not good enough, or maybe, just maybe:

YOU'RE LOVING THE WRONG PERSON.

Love is something you share because you have it, not something you give desperately because you need it. The first person on the top of your love list should be (drum roll... the suspense is killing me...) YOURSELF.

If someone isn't appreciating the love you send their way, then there needs to come a point that you wake up, get up, and walk away; not to make them miss you, but so you can recapture your self dignity and worth.

I've said it numerous times, and I'm going to say it again, if you don't love yourself, you have no business seeking love from others. Other people will exploit your need for love and affection for their own benefit, don't hold that against them, just stay away from them.

If these words are hitting home, don't pity yourself, love yourself, and put yourself in the situation you deserve to be in.

Love is something you share
because you have it, not
something you give desperately
because you need it.

HOW WE SPEND OUR DAYS BECOMES OUR LIFE

Your priorities are not revealed in your words, they are revealed in your actions, and your actions are revealed by your schedule.

You can say something (or someone) is important to you, but if they aren't penciled in, you're lying to yourself.

Tomorrow is not a promise, not even kind of. If fear is holding you back from doing what you want (or need) to be doing in your life just realize that fear isn't going anywhere, and everyone who has done something amazing has done it despite the fear, not in its absence.

Until science can do otherwise, we're all ending our story with death. It's really up to you how you use the days leading up to your eventual demise. The thought of death scares some, and makes others feel liberated. I like to remember, as long as there's breath in my lungs I can create any life I wish to create (it won't be easy, but nothing worth while is), and once the breath is gone, it doesn't matter anyways.

Life is too short to be in any situation you don't want to be in, and it feels even shorter when you're with people you don't want to be around. There aren't any erasers to undo our past, but there are fresh pages to write a new chapter. I have great friends that mustered up the courage and strength to escape their comfort zones and place themselves in a situation they would much rather be in. It took time and it was a struggle, but they came out as better people with better lives. You can do the same thing. It won't be easy, but so what, is there really a point of building a life if it isn't the life you want?

I strongly encourage you to take risks; you're worth it. The fear isn't going to go away, so respect that relationship, and work with it, around it, and despite it.

Let your actions do the talking from now on, and if something is important to you let it show in your day-to-day movements.

Life is too short to be in any situation you don't want to be in, or to be with or around people you don't want to be around.

11
PUTTING YOURSELF FIRST
IS NOT SELFISH

We all see this world in terms of ourselves. We all have interests and needs that need to be met first. This isn't selfish. Selfish is when you don't allow others to do their own thing and expect them to conform to what you want. You don't want people restricting how you get to live your life so don't do it to others.

Focusing on yourself is really one of the least selfish things you can do. It puts you in a position to be empathetic to other people who are also trying to focus on themselves. You can develop an "Imma do me, you do you" mindset, which can create an environment to let people grow on their own terms (scary idea for control freaks).

Instead of trying to find that right person for you, focus on becoming that right person yourself. The people you appreciate will generally be the people who appreciate you so be around them and work on being the type of person you want around.

Putting yourself first is an act of survival as well. We can all easily drain ourselves trying to accommodate to the whims of others. We can spend our entire life trying to make other people happy, and realize we have no life left for ourselves.

It's not romantic to think about how really self-indulgent we all are, but that doesn't take away from that fact. If you understand that people work according to their interests, it's even easier to work with them and get along. Everyone wants to know what's in it for them, respect this ideal, and everyone will benefit from the interactions.

Selfish isn't pursuing what you want in life, it's when you're not also helping others in theirs. We all have things and people we're enthusiastic about, help them, and find joy in doing so. I'm a product of all your support and appreciate you all for it. I'm not in a position to help everyone nor am I motivated to do so, so I focus on those I can and want to help. Social obligations, and being around people you don't want to be around, are just a waste of life.

It's OK to let people know that you're not excited to be around them, if anything, that'll keep you from having to be around them for much longer.

Instead of trying to find that right person for you, focus on becoming that right person yourself.

12 WHEN WAS THE WORLD FAIR?

The world isn't fair, never was, never will be.

To expect reciprocity for being a good person is like sticking your hand in the cage of a lioness and expecting her not to bite your arm off, because after all, you wouldn't do that to her.

If you want to be a good person, be a good person. If you want to be just, treat all fairly, and live in peace and harmony, go right ahead. However, please do not think that these lifestyle choices ensure or entitle you to the same in return.

Only in the movies do the good guys win; by that I mean only in the movies do we actually have good guys. In the real world, things cannot be simplified into good and bad so easily. Almost every privilege we have is at the result of the exploitation of others. If the quality of life you are afforded, you being the person who has electricity and Internet access to read this, was provided to everyone on the planet, we would need a few extra planets. Our nature has become one of abundance and consumption, and that way of life, as 15,000 years of human history has shown, doesn't come without a few cracked skulls.

The point I'm here to make isn't one of pessimism, but more realism. Most of the problems the inhabitants of this planet are experiencing are caused by its inhabitants (well not the bunny rabbits, or dolphins, or scorpions, mostly the humans). Before we start solving these problems, we have to stop causing them, thus no longer benefiting from them. Everyone is guided by self interests, and on top of that, those interests are so different. These interests not only overlap, but conflict with others, like those silly

Iraqis who somehow stumbled upon OUR oil. Conflicting interests leads to conflict. Conflict can lead to death, and when humans are involved, death is the least of the creative things we concoct when dealing with individuals that stand in our way. Humans aren't the only creatures that exhibit war and murderous behavior; we've just spent the most time towards perfecting that art.

Now maybe we're all just not praying hard enough, or sinning too much, and our endlessly loving lord is showing the errors of our ways through intense, but loved filled acts of violence, famine, and other non-pleasantries. Maybe it's the devil (who by most accounts is a fallen angel), or maybe we should pay a bit more attention when we watch the nature channel and see the baby antelope get eaten alive by a pack of lions, and see in them what we so greatly wish to ignore in ourselves.

Most of us are fortunate not to be in geographical locations or economic scenarios that land us on the front lines of humanities worst. That's something I try not to forget, and it's a point I'm grateful for.

Sikh heritage promotes individuals stay armed and trained for combat at all times, regardless if they're men, women or children. In all combat, understanding your terrain is essential (word to Sun Tzu). Folks like, 50 Cent, and the homey, Ryan Blair, were able to take their embedded understanding of the harsh terrain of street life, and apply it to their business ventures. They both found success working with the challenges instead of against them. These are two individuals you won't hear complain, instead you'll witness them adapt until they conquer.

The strongest don't survive, the most adaptable do. When life is viewed this way nothing is seen as an obstruction, but merely an obstacle to overcome.

"Be like water making its way through cracks. Do not be assertive, but adjust to the object, and you shall find a way around or through it. If nothing within you stays rigid, outward things will disclose themselves.

Empty your mind, be formless. Shapeless, like water. If you put water into a cup, it becomes the cup. You put water into a bottle and it becomes the bottle. You put it in a teapot, it becomes the teapot. Now, water can flow or it can crash. Be water, my friend."
– Bruce Lee

The better our relationship is with reality, the better we can get along and live together. It may not be pretty, but it's all we have.

The strongest don't survive,
the most adaptable do.

13

YOU'RE GOING TO DIE

Also, everyone you love and care for will be dead within a dozen decades, some even before you. Why does thinking about that bother us so much?

What other guarantees do we have in life besides death? When folks die, how do we determine if they went too early? Is it based on the average? Does it even make sense to quantify life in terms of time?

"It's not the days in your life, but the life in your days."

For many of us, there is a disconnect in our relationship with death. We tend to forget that our days are not promised. Every day you receive is a gift, whether you die at the age of five or 50, every millisecond of that existence was never assured. I'm not sure where the idea that we're entitled to life came from. Our only real entitlement is that it's going to come to an end.

I don't see this as depressing, but rather the opposite.

The beauty of life is that it's temporary, and if it lasted forever we'd take it for granted. Many folks are already taking it for granted, as if it will last forever.

Respecting mortality will dramatically enhance how efficiently we spend the time we have here. It also keeps us from sweating the small stuff (when you compare it to death, all of it is small stuff). I think our innate urges to create come from our desires to be immortal. Similar to religion; many of those beliefs revolve around the idea of what happens after we die, and what we need to do beforehand to ensure an awesome afterlife (it's great marketing if you think about it; you won't know if it's bullsh*t until after you're dead, and by then it's too late to get your time and money back).

Personally, I see us as just another cell in Mama Nature. Like the cells in our bodies, new cells are created, and old cells die, all serving whatever purpose nature has them programmed for. Mother Nature does a great job of monkey-butlering us to do her bidding without us even knowing. On top of that, we tend to think we're still in control while doing it (like bees pollinating flowers).

It's just a view, but most of the things that affect us are based on the views we hold, and our view on death is an important one to meditate on.

Paying attention to our relationship with death is also a great exercise in letting go. Sikh Philosophy encourages detachment, and it's pretty practical advice if you think about it. Our attachment to people, things, ideas, and beliefs can be quite a cause of misery for the short time period we actually have. Everything is temporary, there's really no need to hold on.

I don't concern myself with ideas of the supernatural and afterlife, but I do understand why those ideas are appealing. We want to believe there's more than what's in front of us, more than just the lights shutting off. The fear of the unknown can compel us to various mindsets.

Regardless, the lights will be going out in all of us, and that's not a choice. However, HOW we feel about that IS a choice. Let's enjoy what we have, while we have it, and not spend it worrying about a future we may never see or an ending we can't avoid.

We're all going to die, and for me, that's what makes life worth living. The fact that the folks I love and care about are going to share that fate is motivation to enjoy their company and not take it for granted while I have them.

And when it's time:
"Don't cry because it's over. Smile because it happened." - Dr. Seuss

Let's enjoy what we have, while we have it, and not spend it worrying about a future we may never see or an ending we can't avoid.

14 WHO ARE YOU?

No one will ever know you better than yourself. No one else should have the power to define you more than yourself. Seeking approval from others allows them dominion over your identity.

The outside world will never have a great picture of what's inside; WE barely know. Our opinions of our indentity aren't always valid or accurate either, but they definitely affect how we feel about ourselves.

Closing your eyes, shutting the f*ck up and exploring what's inside is a great way of getting a firm grasp of who's really there. That picture will never be captured in a camera and can never be validated by the people around you.

As Dr. Suess says, "Why try to fit in, when you were born to stand out." There is no normal, and what's considered common isn't common everywhere (the more you travel, the more you'll realize that). If people don't like you for who you are, change the people, not yourself.

If people don't like you for who you are, change the people, not yourself.

15 WE ALL HAVE OUR STRESSES

Fear, anxiety, loneliness, discomfort, pain, jitters, or whatever you're going through is an expensive experience.

It can f*ck with your health, your mood, your motivation, and productivity. It can even mess with your ability to be around other people.

I can't promise to make it feel better. There are plenty of crooks that you can throw your money at for that. What I can promise is this: you have limitless power to make that sh*t even worse.

Comparison is the thief of joy, and if you're having a rough patch, looking at the lives of others will not help. Everyone is going through what they're going through, but many still get up and keep their lives moving, those folks are called adults. Observing everyone on the surface, then comparing what you see to what you're feeling deep inside, is a guaranteed method of sinking yourself even lower.

This is not to say find consolation in the fact that others have bullsh*t as well, but more to realize that just maybe bullsh*t is a just part of life. Life doesn't start after the obstacles; life is the obstacles.

A carefree, stress-free, all problems get solved within 22 minutes type of life ONLY exists on television. To begin with, most of the things we call problems aren't even problems, they're dilemmas. These dilemmas are generally attributed to our ample leisure time in the first world. Folks in other situations rarely have the luxury to ponder or stress on many of things we do, mainly because they're too busy surviving (cue Jim Jeffries singing "Don't Die Today").

It's not my place to evaluate the things that keep you up at night, or cause you anxiety. I have, however, realized in my time on this planet, that outside actual death (and a few other exceptions), the intensity of our problems is the simple marriage of our circumstance with our mindset. Sometimes you can't change the circumstances, but you can ALWAYS change your mindset (if at this point you said, "Easier said than done Humble," you owe me $5).

Death itself is the one sure shot promise so there's really no point in worrying about that. We all have that in common.

I'm not writing this for you, I'm writing this for me. My molars hurt because I've been grinding my teeth in my sleep. It's a sign of stress. From what? A bunch of stuff and people that won't matter in 90 years and rarely exist in my present. It's the memories of a past and fears of the future causing that stress. Anything that isn't in the present are simply products of my imagination (downside to the over-thinker)

No empathy needed, it's what we all go through. It's uncomfortable, but that's where growth lives.

There's no growth in your comfort zone, there's no comfort in your growth zone. It's not a Venn diagram and there's no happy medium.

Whatever you're going through, go through it, learn from it, and grow from it. You won't be here forever.

Life doesn't start after the obstacles; life is the obstacles.

16 PAVE YOUR OWN ROAD, THERE'S LESS TRAFFIC

Many of us define our successes in seeing what other people have. As a rapper, I can pick a handful of artists whose careers I want to emulate. That's cool, it's healthy to aspire, but usually we can fall into the trap of trying to follow a beaten path.

Now this isn't a hipster mindset of being original (which ends up being even less original), it's more of an understanding that it's in our nature to find the path of least resistance. If someone found success creating a certain path, you can be sure that path will be clogged with people trying to follow in their footsteps.

When you pave your own road, there's less traffic.

Now our goals are all pretty much the same. We want to (insert some goal) so we can be happy. Many of us have achieved goals only to still remain unfulfilled, and so we create new goals. This repetitive exercise can keep us busy until we die.

Today I had an awesome conversation with an awesome friend who has been traveling around the globe in pursuit of his happiness. I told him about the bazillion things I have going on and he asked, "What do you want life to be." I didn't have to think about it, I replied, "I want to be able to ride my bike everyday and bring my ideas to life," he then told me to stop doing everything that doesn't help me get on that bike and bring those ideas to life.

The beauty of that conversation was that he prompted me to share my very unique vision of happy. It's a much different view of, "I want to be rich and famous," because a lot of people want to be rich and famous. We're all saying the same thing though, "I want to be happy, and this is what I think will get me there." For me, happiness is sunshine, pretty girls, bike rides, and creativity. That requires some money for the bills, but I can skip all the other bullsh*t that comes with the rat race.

I think the more unique and clear your happy vision is, the more clear and unique the path you need to pave to get there will be. Happy visions will change as time goes on because our priorities will change. What was important to you when you were 10, changed when you were 15, changed again when you were 20, and will change again when you're 25, 30, 35, etc. Don't be too attached to them.

Also realize if you don't choose to find happiness with what you have, you won't find happiness with what you get. That's how I see ambition, and that's cool too. We can find peace in the fact that there won't ever be peace as well.

The more you know yourself, the more unique your adventure will be for you. There's no need to follow the herd; what makes them smile won't necessarily be right for you.

Because you take the time to read my sh*t, I wish nothing but the best for you; I hope you have a happy vision and wake up with energy to chase it 1000% every day.

There's no need to follow
the herd, what makes them
smile won't necessarily
be right for you.

17 DON'T SABOTAGE YOURSELF

Often, our biggest obstacle in life is simply ourselves. Our mind can use its creative powers to give us plenty to worry about and fear. Those worries and fears can serve to prevent us from moving forward in life.

In our need to avoid suffering, we'll tend to stick to the comfortable things, whether they're in our best interest or not. This is particularly common in relationships. The transition of letting people go, and attempting to seek out new people can be very daunting. We can easily decide to avoid any of those activities, and just stick with what we have, because after all it's what we know and are used to (comfort).

If you know what you want from life, don't let anyone tell you that it can't be obtained, especially if the one telling you is yourself. We only allow others to speak to us a certain way if it matches with the thoughts and feelings we already have.

Don't let others put you down, and DEFINITELY do not put yourself down. It's a pointless act; if you recognize something in yourself you feel needs improvement, don't wallow in self-pity, improve it.

As always, this is easier said than done, I'm not here to sell you easy, I'm here to remind you what you always knew needed to be done, and I'm just letting you know it's worth the effort, you're worth the effort.

The moment you realize that your thoughts have such a dramatic impact on your mood, being, and ability to function, is the same moment you can begin to shift those thoughts to improve things.

In Sikh Pholosophy, Baba Nanak wrote, "Man Jeetay, Jag Jeet," which means, "Conquered Mind, Conquered World".

It's amazing how well we function in the outside world, when we're control of our world inside.

We only allow others to speak to us a certain way if it matches with the thoughts and feelings we already have.

TIME HEALS ALL, BUT NOT ON YOUR SCHEDULE

Random things trigger bad memories; memories of an ex or lost one; memories of a tragic experience; memories of a missed opportunity; and those triggers remind you that you're not completely over it.

All you can do in those moments is remind yourself, that pain can only exist because you're in the past. The past doesn't exist anymore, and that pain is as real as you allow it to be. You can combat that by focusing on the only thing you have, the present.
Snow melting, leaves growing, people aging, all happen at a pace that wasn't designed to fit our patience level. Our patience and attention span continues to dwindle as our technological culture pushes more towards the need for immediate gratification.

The natural pace of things will NEVER accommodate you so maybe you could take steps to accommodate it. Doing things to speed up the process may do the opposite. Don't try to numb the pain that may just delay the healing.

Focus on your relationship with yourself, and what you need to improve from the situation you're in. No one knows what's best for you better than yourself. There's a lot of awesomeness hiding inside, all you have to do is explore.

You're not allowing time to take its course; time doesn't require your permission. Instead you're respecting time, and saving yourself grief in the process.

Don't try to numb the pain
that may just delay the healing.

A LESSON FROM 50 CENT

When I started this music journey, my content was so idealistic. I wanted to cure the ails of the world through rhyming on beats.

Then I started researching a bit deeper, and realized that the ugliness that exists on our planet is rarely an accident. There are always more than two sides of the coin. I learned that simple minds simplify things as purely good and bad, except it's a lot more ying-yang.

That's when I divorced idealism and starting flirting with realism. My only goal now is to understand things rather than evaluate them like I have any position or authority to judge.

It's called the REAL WORLD for a reason. Take the time to observe and soak it up. You have to learn as you go; there won't be a wrap up at the end with a summarizing song and dance.

Thinking you already have it figured out closes your windows to a universe of learning opportunities and growth.

That's what I learned from 50 cent:
"I'ma absorb everything that's going on, and take what I can get from it. Ain't no school for this sh*t stupid! You gotta be smart enough to pick up the information as you go."

Clearly he doesn't have my charm, but the lesson is just as valuable and has changed me for the better.

Thanks Fif.

"Ain't no school for this sh*t stupid! You gotta be smart enough to pick up the information as you go."

20 YOU CAN BE WHATEVER THE F*CK YOU WANT

Remember the rule: Whenever you read something I write, and say, "Easier said than done," you owe me $5. Why the f*ck would it be easy, difficulty is what makes it worth it.

In life, if you don't know who you are, there will be entities, systems, and people to tell you who you are. Media will subtly jam into your brain, what you should look like, smell like, act like, talk like, walk like, and like in general. Even if you have a very unique concept of yourself, it's not set in stone.

What it means to be a man, woman, citizen, rapper, celebrity, student, employee, etc., are all constructions of society. Nature is a minor factor, and only once mixed with your nurture does your definition begin to form. We are all a mixture of our nature and nurture; the more we discover those elements, the better we can work at our redesigns.

People make a horrible mistake of assuming elements of their personality or core-being as somehow purely genetic, or in their blood. The reality is you're not married to who you are, you can change it any moment, the change may not be overnight, but nothing about you is concrete; it's a construct. Anything that is constructed can be destroyed.

The idea that we're too old to change is ridiculous. The truth is, the older we get, the less folks we have to answer to, thus the less we need to adapt and change. Someone who thinks they're unable to adapt and change just needs to spend some time in prison, or any other circumstance where their privileges of stagnation are no longer afforded.

Just because you have the power to be whatever you want, doesn't mean you can be whatever you want. Many of the things we want to be are still ideas fed to us. It's a tricky balance of paying attention to your insides and the outside around you.

One thing's for sure; the most celebrated individuals are the ones that amplify their unique characteristics. Even cookie cutter personalities came from an original stencil. When I see folks in the creative fields, some feed off trends, while others create the trends that are fed off.

I work hard to be a stencil.

It's about creating and destroying yourself on a regular basis. Every version of yourself serves it's purpose, and killing that self for the new self is a great exercise in letting go and avoiding comfort zones. Comfort zones, after all, are the enemy of growth

It also keeps us excited for the days ahead. The goal in 5 years is to look back at the present me, and be happy I'm no longer here.

What parts of you need to be fed? What parts need to be starved, and killed off?

We are all a mixture of our nature and nurture, the more we discover those elements, the better we can work at our redesigns.

21
LONELY IS A FEELING, NOT A CIRCUMSTANCE

Sometimes it may have nothing to do with a lack of company, but rather a wall we put up ourselves.

The fear of loneliness can drive us to compromise who we are, thinking it will open us up to other people. The reality is, we're only further trapping our true selves in a shell of someone else. That furthers us from our most important relationship, the one with our self.

The more time we spend getting to know ourselves, the better equipped we'll be to determine our compatibility with others. It will also make us less dependent on others to fill a void, allowing us to have healthy relationships based on more than simply quelling our fear of loneliness.

You can feel lonely in a crowded room, or at peace in secluded solitude. Depending on others to determine that can be a fickle game; relationships die and change like the seasons.

Love yourself before you concern yourself with the love of others. Love when you're ready, not when you're lonely.

Love when you're ready,
not when you're lonely

22 DON'T TRUST EVERYTHING YOU FEEL

We're all unique in our own way, especially the way we react to different situations. It's not really a debate of nature versus nurture, but more a question of how your nature and nurture work together to create the person you are.

Because we all have different experiences and unique wiring, that mixture can make it difficult for us to understand what we feel, why we feel it, and why no one else in the room is feeling the same thing.

I'm not sure if any other creature spends as much time living in the past and future as we do. As our mind travels between the two non-existent realms, our feelings travel with them. The feelings we attach to these times, especially the not-so-pleasant feelings can be damaging and not worth experiencing, considering they're related to places that either no longer exist or have yet to occur.

Most recently, I began to focus more time on figuring out WHY I was experiencing the emotions I felt, rather than simply accepting them. This did wonders for how I dealt with things that came my way.

A lot of stress and anxiety comes from thinking about the future, and the dreaded what if scenarios that race through your head, creating a paralyzing fear, keeping us from creating moments drenched in our potential.

There's plenty of regret and depression that comes from dwelling in the past, repeatedly focusing on the coulda-woulda-shouldas of life. This practice ignores the simple fact that the times reminisced don't exist, and outside of learning from past events, they're pointless to revisit.

Sometimes the things we're feeling at the moment have nothing to do with the moment. Instead, they're related solely to another time. We end up wasting today focusing on yesterday, or worrying about tomorrow. The simple fact is: the present is all we have.

I met a friend from high school a few days back. He, like myself, has left the comfort and security of a steady paycheck to pursue his passions. He talked to me about the fears of f*cking up and how all he has to do to quell those fears is to remind himself to stop getting in his own way. Our minds have the power to both help and harm us; it's up to us to use that power wisely.

We don't always have the power to change our circumstances, but we can change how we feel about them. Happiness is a feeling, not a destination. If you rely on a circumstance or outcome to be happy, then that dependence will only grow into an addiction. You'll be climbing a mountain without a peak, feeling more and more hollow the higher you get.

Just because you're feeling down, doesn't mean you have to be down. Have a conversation with yourself and figure out the root of the emotion. It's very unlikely it has anything to do with where you are in the exact present moment. We busy ourselves to get our mind off things. That act in itself brings us back into the present with a task that requires us to focus on the here and now.

Emotions are a crazy phenomenon, especially the idea of love. There was a cool TED talk that discussed the concept of love being an apparatus of nature used to ensure we coexist long enough to reproduce, ensuring the continuity of our species and nothing more.

Whether you agree with that concept is up to you. Although, I do hope that the idea motivates you to take time to consider WHY you feel what you feel. Some think feelings can't be rationalized, they can however, be identified and related to root causes and events. Understanding what triggers your emotions will definitely put you in a better situation to deal with them as they come. It's all about taking the time to get to know yourself and your unique modes of functions.

We don't always have the
power to change our
circumstances, but we
can change how we
feel about them.

23 THINGS GET OVERWHELMING QUICKLY

Then the anxiety builds, and we freeze. Because we freeze, less gets done. Because less gets done, more piles up. Because more piles up, anxiety builds [repeat].

The anxiety comes from our imagination's idea of the things we need to do. Getting them done comes from the baby steps we take to get the things in motion.

The remedy to this anxiety is taking the first step, laying the first brick, standing up from your chair, and remembering getting anything done is better than doing nothing.

The tiny stuff adds up. Stay focused on your journey one step at a time; there's so much to learn and experience along the way.

Also, don't forget to breathe. Take a deep breath, relax, and slow it down to avoid being conquered by worry.

...getting anything done is better than doing nothing.

24 I DON'T KNOW YOU

But like most people I encounter, you have aspirations. Those aspirations may be anything from making rent, to owning a Ferrari for every day of the week. The specifics of your aspirations are irrelevant. Actually your entire dream is pointless if you don't plan on pulling that trigger and making it happen.

We can do an awesome job sabotaging ourselves with excuses and reasons not to make things happen. Sometimes we trick ourselves into thinking we're going to make it happen soon. Soon being starting tomorrow, next week, next month, as soon as I have time, as soon as I have enough money, once my kids are grown. These abstract moments never arrive, but we feel like they will.

In my experience, you just need to shut the f*ck up and START. No proclamations, no "as soon as...", and no delays. Just get started. Whatever you're afraid of is dramatically worse in your mind, and it doesn't hold any weight in reality.

Whatever great ideas you have are worthless and pointless until they marry an execution (even in business, you can't copyright an idea, just the method of its execution). The secret to success is not having a magical idea, but realizing that you are the key executioner that can't be copied if anyone tried. There is no one like you on this rock, there never was, and after you're gone there won't be anyone like you again. That makes you one in 100 billion. As a unique being, what can you accomplish and contribute during your limited moments on Earth?

There are people accomplishing amazing things everyday, and very little of it is luck. Most of it comes from an unfathomable amount of work that you rarely hear about. When we witness these accomplishments, we have a couple of choices. We can drown in envy, and console ourselves with excuses as to why that can't be us (or even worse, why it shouldn't even be them), or we can see their accomplishments as evidence that things beyond the norm are completely within your reach. You'll notice the pattern that most change comes from a change in your mind before anything else in the outside world.

I released my first tape in March 2009. Every track, rhyme, performance, post, mistake, and release is a baby step towards my aspirations. It all starts with a single step. You don't need to know every step in your dreams, you just need to START. In 90 years you'll be dead anyways, what do you really have to lose?

Once you start moving, all those limitations and ideas of impossible fade. It's not going to be easy, but nothing worth accomplishing ever is.

Most of my progress began the moment I began believing in myself more than anyone else. I have a feeling it'll be the same for you. No more excuses.

What are your aspirations, and what are you going to do to get started?

Once you start moving, all those limitations and ideas of impossible fade. It's not going to be easy, but nothing worth accomplishing ever is.

25   HUKAM

In Sikhi, there's a concept of Hukam.

Some folks interpret that as the "will of the supreme," which is to be accepted, and not questioned. Personally, I understand it as the nature of things, which is to be understood and worked with.

Don't submit to the wind nor complain and fight it. Rather, adjust to it. You can only adjust to the wind if you understand it. Learn as much as you can about the REAL world and the mechanisms that govern it; that will best prepare you to adapt and maneuver in life to achieve what you want.

Before you can concern yourself with how you WANT it to be, you have to understand how it IS. How it IS can't be taught to you, it has to be experienced and explored. Once you strengthen your relationship with reality, you'll be able to bend the spoon a lot easier (If you don't get the reference, we can't be friends).

Remember, the strongest don't survive, the most adaptable do.

Before you can concern yourself with how you WANT it to be, you have to understand how it IS.

26 MONEY IS A FUNNY THING

A lot of people who don't have money either worship it or downplay its value. Some of those who do have it in abundance either take it for granted or use it as their scorecard to move ahead in life.

Money is a tool. It's a resource. People should not downplay resources; we need them, we want them, we spend much of our waking moments in pursuit of them. If the world were one big library, where people borrowed and returned resources on the honour system, we wouldn't need money, but that isn't the case.

Money is what you make it. People call money the root of all evil, but I think Mark Twain got it right when he said, "The LACK of money is the root of all evil." The problem with a word such as lack is that it can mean anything. We all live beyond our means. Many of the things we consider are needs, are still luxuries when compared to how the majority of the world is living. There are families living on less than a dollar a day, and I read a story of a farmer in India who committed suicide because it would have taken him 90 years to pay back an outstanding loan of $300USD.

Money is a made up concept, but everyone's playing along. Money can do well to stay in your head, but can cause problems when it finds its way into your heart. Ambitious folks are never satisfied, and will accumulate until their number is called. Content folks have no need, and can find happiness and peace in whatever their situation may be.

I know I'm happier wanting less than getting more. I'm not an idealist though, and understand the nature of this planet, and the importance resources play into that. Ever since we learned to hold, we learned to own, and once we learned to own, the rat race began.

Never confuse greed and ambition; greedy folks want it without acknowledging or respecting the work that it takes to get it.

Your relationship with money is yours and yours alone. Don't allow others to dictate what it means or doesn't mean to you. My wealth is my family and friends, and I dream of being in a position financially to make their dreams come true.

What does it mean for you?

I know I'm happier wanting
less than getting more.

27
A FEAR OVERCOME IS A STRENGTH ACQUIRED.

What's the point of existing in such a diverse realm if all we're going to do is huddle with those that look, act, talk, walk, and think like us.

Relationships aren't successful based on common interests. They're successful when they're based on common priorities. If your priority is to learn and grow, your potential pool of experiences grows exponentially.

These days I don't mind standing out and I don't avoid discomfort. Folks can stare; it's great practice for me to make eye contact and smile. The last time I did that at a concert I met a white dude that just spent four months in Chandigarh, and he was only staring because he was excited to see a Punjabi. Another time, I was at a Toronto Raptors game and this dude just wanted to know how long I had been "working on that beard."

Also, I'm Punjabi, we have our own staring problems.

Get out there. Be uncomfortable. Make mistakes. Get embarrassed. We'll all be dead soon, it's not a big deal.

Get out there.
Be uncomfortable.
Make mistakes.
Get embarrassed.
We'll all be dead soon,
it's not a big deal.

28 TRUST YOUR WINGS

There's a popular saying that when a bird sits on a branch they don't depend on the branch not to snap, but rather depend on their own wings to keep them safe. The vast majority of the universe is out of our control, and that simple reason is why our dependence should not be on it, but rather on ourselves. No one can promise you a life void of suffering and hard times, and it's probably a better bet to promise yourself the exact opposite.

We don't know and can't control many of our circumstances, but we are in control of the efforts and the choices we can make to deal with them. Putting faith in your wings is only logical if you train those muscles, and muscles are best strengthened with resistance and stability training. This naturally comes with time; the older we get, the more we've seen, and the less things feel like a big deal. The first heartbreak seems the worst, but it better equips us for the next relationship. If you're reading this and have yet to have your heart ripped out of your chest, be grateful when it does. There's much to learn and grow from such an excruciating experience.

We sometimes get so caught up worrying about the branches snapping, and we lose sight of our abilities to adapt to such circumstances and come out OK if it actually occurs. I read a quote that says, "Worrying is like paying a down payment on a problem you may never have."

I'm not asking you to have faith that things will all work out for the best, that's too idealistic for someone who's actually paying attention to the world around them. What I am asking is for you to have faith in yourself and your abilities to deal with whatever challenges will surely come your way.

As someone who performs in front of many people, my anxieties about being in front of the public mainly dwindle with my faith in my preparation. If I'm prepared, I feel much better about what I'm going to do than if I have to wing it. It's cliché to say, but makes a lot of sense, "Hope for the best, prepare for the worst." Even when things are going well, be prepared for the worst case scenarios, it will cushion the blow if something happens. You don't need to trust a world you can't control, just trust yourself to do your best to get through it.

You don't need to trust a
world you can't control, just
trust yourself to do your
best to get through it

20 YOU HAVE REASONS TO BE MISERABLE

You also have reasons to smile.

I don't know the specifics of any of those reasons, circumstances, or situations, but I do know that you get to decide what you want to focus on.

It's very easy to ignore all the things going according to plan, and to zero in on the things that aren't meeting our expectations. This is making a conscious choice and wasting valuable calories being miserable. When we make such a decision, our mood can snowball into a dark place, and all of a sudden all other pain begins to amplify as well. It's what's commonly referred to as a *downward spiral*.

Making a conscious decision to be happy may require nothing more than deciding on paying attention to the awesome things that are happening in your life. You can start with something as simple as this: you're f*cking breathing, and somehow the sack of meat, you call a body, uses each breath to feed your blood, which in turn keeps the things in your body working (including the eyes and brain you need to read this).
People who focus on things they're thankful for will generally be happier. This process can begin with a list of everything you're grateful for and you can start that right now.

No seriously... start now.

Some of you reading this may feel miserable, and may not even want to try something like a gratitude list because you're scared. After feeling a certain pain for an extended period of time we may fool ourselves to believe that this pain is part of who we are, and that foolish belief can prevent us from taking steps to remedy that pain.

I can promise you 11 times out of 10 that the only change and growth you can have comes from breaking a cycle, and putting yourself in a new position, which is generally uncomfortable. Don't fear the discomfort. When you were a baby first crawling there was a discomfort. When you learned to walk, run, ride a bike, read, and write there was a discomfort. Don't deny yourself the opportunity for a better life simply because you're scared to roll up your sleeves and do some work.

We tend to sabotage our happiness by ignoring the wonderful things in our life. It's a martyr syndrome, where we confuse self-pity for self-love. Nothing worthwhile comes from feeling sorry for yourself. That self pity only isolates you from the beauty and catalyst of happiness around you.

Personally, when I feel miserable, I look for creative art and images that leave me in awe and inspire me to create. Sometimes I press play on music, put on headphones, and dance it off. Other times I put my face in the Sun, close my eyes, take a deep breath, and tell myself, "Suck it up, let's keep it movin'," then get back to work.

There are plenty of reasons to be miserable and there are plenty of reasons to be happy. Decide what you want in your life, and realize the responsibility for how you feel lies solely with you.

We tend to sabotage our
happiness by ignoring the
wonderful things in our life

30 FLUFFY PILLOWS AND THE TRUTH

You know that feeling early in the morning when you hear the alarm (or your mom yelling) and you have to make that critical decision whether to get your ass up or bury your face back into that soft pillow, and stay wrapped under the warm blanket (or as Homer Simpson so poetically puts it, "...a warm cinnamon bun").

Then all of a sudden, reality hits (or your mom keeps yelling) and you jerk yourself out of bed because you know that, as comfortable as that bed is, you must part ways to start the adventures of your day; because fortunately and unfortunately, there are more important things in the world than staying in bed

That relationship to our pillow is really no different to the many other relationships we have in our lives. We can call this our comfort zone, and like our pillow, there isn't much to benefit from remaining in our comfort zone as the world keeps turning. In our own history, most of our personal growth and triumphs usually come when we've found ourselves out of pocket in situations that weren't familiar, and even sometimes scary. Many times we were forced into, or stumbled upon these circumstances, and the growth came from adapting or digging ourselves out.

For my folks who have spent a few decades on this planet, that may have been their first (second, third or forth) heartbreak, for others maybe it was adjusting to high school, getting fired, moving to another city, or the loss of a loved one.

For me most recently I realized my comfort zone wasn't a zone at all, but more of a frequency, and that it wasn't even about my world, but more to do with HOW I was choosing to take in the world around me.

I pride myself in being an honest individual and I try to say it like it is, but I quickly realized more important than SAYING it like it is, I first needed to SEE it as it is. Though I was speaking the truth, I still wasn't always comfortable realizing it. I realized my lust for lies after having being taken advantage of a few too many occasions. Those occasions happened because I was being told what I wanted to hear, even if the stories defied my most basic common sense.

Comforting lies are those fluffy pillows, while harsh realities are those cold showers. When we listen to politicians talk out their asses, making promises and statements that fact checkers immediately refute, we fail to realize that even they don't concern themselves with ensuring the accuracy of their statements; they're concerned with the appeal of it. People don't care if Obama didn't close Guantanamo, or bombed Pakistan more than Bush; he's telling folks what they want to hear, and that is more valuable than bringing those promises to fruition. It's affirmation over information.

We all think they can't get one over on us, that we don't get suckered in by advertisement, and that they exist and all that marketing money spent on commercials is for those other chumps. The truth is, we're all chumps. Even our relationships with others can be based primarily on how they make us feel about ourselves. The comfort of hearing what we want will always be there. That urge is exploited and we're massaged ever so gently into a certain direction, which is beneficial to the ones feeding us the lies, even when we're lying to ourselves.

Another reason we find comfort in deception is in the beauty of its simplicity. The truth is rarely simple, and generally deals with 10 different shades of grey. All our tired minds want to hear is the black and white version. The truth can be complex, complex isn't comforting, so dumb it down, package it, and tell me what to think.

"She's not that into you"; "This activity isn't helping you achieve your goals"; "Even though you've known him your whole life, he's toxic, and you need to cut him loose"; are the types of conversations we have inside that pull us off the pillow and throw us in the shower so we can move forward with our life. You can call it your inner voice, your gut instincts, God, the Spaghetti Monster in your tummy, the voice of reason, or whatever you want; just pay attention to it. The more unsettling it feels, the more you know it's a truth you've been avoiding to hear.

Comforting lies are those fluffy pillows, while harsh realities are those cold showers.

31 IS IT IGNORANCE OR APATHY?

For those that may not know the difference

Ignorance = I DON'T KNOW
Apathy = I DON'T CARE

When people discuss events like hate crimes, the word ignorance gets thrown around. There's this assumption that if people were only educated a bit more on the difference, events that happen towards people who are different wouldn't.

I've walked to the Bronx, and a little boy walked up to me and said, "A Salaam Alaikum." He didn't have the education to realize I wasn't of Islamic heritage, but that ignorance is irrelevant to the fact that the boy was showing me love. This boy was simply looking for a way to connect.

Education is only valuable to those who want to learn and expand their minds. That's where apathy is the culprit. The issue isn't that people don't know, it's that they don't care to know.

When the media has already demonized and sensationalized a group of people, the vast majority of the population will accept it for face value. There isn't critical thinking or discourse, nor is there a desire to do so.

I have little faith that an awareness program is going to change the mind of someone looking to exude their own justice on those who are different. There is a lot to gain from the people in positions of power, when their population is in a constant state of fear. For those that are considered the *other*, that simply means we have to respect the landscape we're in, be prepared accordingly.

Hate, racism, sexism, war, violence, and all the other ugly acts are useful tools to keep people in order, and for that simple fact, they'll continue to exist. An apathetic mass population that is more concerned with themselves, than others, is what guarantees this.

If we continue to see *us* and *them* there will be *us and them*; even when we stop, others may not. Recognize and respect that fact.

This world is what we make it, and I'm extremely impressed and proud of the way Prabhjot Singh, A professor who was recently attacked in Harlem, responded to his experience:

"Honestly, I can't come up with a better response than simply gratitude... I'm thankful for a few reasons. If they had attacked me any more violently, I may not be awake right now to tell my story. If they had attacked me even half an hour earlier, they would have harmed my wife and one-year-old son. And if they had attacked me anywhere else, I may not have had bystanders there to save me."

We can't control the ignorance or apathy of others, but we can recognize it in ourselves; let's start there.

We can't control the ignorance
or apathy of others, but
we can recognize it in
ourselves; let's start there.

32 COMPARISONS ARE KILLER

We can't be ourselves if we don't know ourselves, and we can't know ourselves, if all we know about who we are, is in comparison to others.

We will never know the problem, bullsh*t, and stresses that others are going through, nor do we need to. What we would be better off doing with that time is exploring who we are on the inside.

I know it's hard, we see everyone around us doing awesome things, it has been engrained into the culture to try and keep up, but really there's nothing to keep up to, and no one to keep up with.

Instead of comparing yourself with others, try connecting yourself with others. The more connections you make, the more you'll learn about the world, and yourself. There's a lot we can learn about ourselves through our relationships with others; they'll bring out sides of us we never knew existed.

If you want to be happy you have to recognize the things in your life worth appreciating. If you're spending all your time finding that in others, instead of yourselves, then nothing but misery can come.

Compare yourself to who you were yesterday, and celebrate your evolution. There's plenty to appreciate in the direction you're headed.

Instead of comparing yourself with others, try connecting yourself with others.

33
HIGH EXPECTATIONS AND LOW PATIENCE

Everyone wants it now, if not yesterday. Entitlement is a key word here. Modern advances have brought us things so rapidly that our patience is shot.

When kids get a certificate for just showing up, good luck telling them to work hard to enjoy the fruits of their labor. In a culture that keeps promoting quick and easy, greatness can be at risk.

You want to lose weight, here's the secret: it's going to take hard work and time to see results, you want double the results, it's going to take twice the hard work and time to see results, don't mistake the simplicity of it for easiness. It's easy to understand, not easy to do.

Things take time, and if you don't have the patience to let things slow cook and form then expect a life continually unfulfilled. It took time to learn how to walk, heal from that first heartbreak, finish school, or accomplish anything else worth accomplishing.

Get started and chip away, luck is nothing more than preparation and opportunity. We all have the ability of greatness in us, and can train those muscles so we can see what our real potential is.

Decide what you want, focus on it, and take the baby steps necessary to get there. Encourage those around you to do the same, and support them any way that you want.

The people that don't want you to succeed are simply projecting their fears and inadequacies on you. If you find yourself being discouraging to others, ask yourself, "What am I afraid of if they succeed."

There wasn't always a light bulb, Internet, car, or microwave. These things were dreamed up and created. There are no rules or boundaries besides the ones you set up yourself. What works for one person may not be what works for another.

I hope someone reads this today and decides to change the course of their life by even one degree; that distance will add up in the long run.

Things take time, and if you don't have the patience to let things slow cook and form then expect a life continually unfulfilled.

34 HELP THOSE YOU LOVE THE WAY YOU LOVE

There's no application process, limited spaces, or dog-eat-dog mentality to simply help someone else. When you want to help yourself it becomes an entirely different story.

Wanting to help someone doesn't require you to establish an organization, and it doesn't require a celebrity endorsement, or even a Facebook page. It only requires you to get up and start helping. I met a photographer at a wedding who donates 50% of his entire salary to those in need. He's not financially; he simply stated, "If I wait till I am, it'll never happen."

Helping isn't simply donating. For some, it can be raising awareness, others it can be attending a protest, or getting your hands dirty on the front line. Everyone has their own definition of what it means to help, and that's OK. The myriad of tasks all makes an impact.

Some folks want to save the rainforest, others want to ensure children have clean drinking water, others want to save the whales, while others want to end violence against women. Some only find inspiration when those in need have something in common with them. Not everyone connects with the hunger situation in Africa, or are even aware the hunger situation is worse in the subcontinent of India, and that's not going to change anytime soon. Whatever cause touches you, do it up, hopefully the ones that don't will have folks on them as well.

I think being selfless is a myth when it comes to helping. We still tend to lean towards the causes and tasks that give us the little fuzzy feeling inside, that's fine. I think it's an issue when we start to impose our views on others. If someone else doesn't share your enthusiasm towards preserving the pyramids, don't bang your fists, just do your thing.

The impact you create is the impact you create. The opinions of others are irrelevant to this. Don't be guilt-tripped into supporting something your heart isn't into. Everyone is guided by self-interests, and though that doesn't sound very romantic, it's still very accurate. Don't feel obligated to cater to the interests of others, handle yours.

Whatever causes you choose to support, please explore it first. There are plenty of scams (like the Kony campaign) that will exploit the suffering of others for profit. The situations are never simple in black and white. There's rarely a clearly defined good guy and bad guy. Get educated, and find the best use of your energy to create impact you want to create.

It doesn't have to be grand; helping folks can be as simple as opening doors, or taking the time to lend an ear, or sharing a smile.

The impact you create is the impact you create. The opinions of others are irrelevant to this.

35 LET'S TALK ABOUT YOUR BELIEFS

At this point, some of you may be thinking (in a Jim Jeffries Voice), "Don't you with f*ck my beliefs Humble, you wrote a few cute things, but you're about to cross the line. Respect my beliefs."

I have every intention to f*ck with your beliefs.
I don't even know your beliefs; I don't really care what they are. I'm more concerned with the idea of beliefs itself.

Beliefs are simply opinions that we don't particularly want to reevaluate. They may pertain to our favourite sports teams, political ideologies, spiritual philosophies, or simply the way we govern our lives.

People take pride in their beliefs, as if having a particular belief is an accomplishment of some sort. This is an interesting idea because once pride enters the ring; folks then relate their beliefs to their identity.

Once people stick the flag of identity into a belief they no longer see a distinction between the belief and themselves. These are the types of individuals that get bent when you criticize their beliefs. At this point I could give specific examples, but that action alone would illustrate my point.

The stronger the belief, the more we're dug in and the less pleasant it is to hear anything that doesn't support that thought. We are bound to facts, but we HOLD beliefs. Sometimes we can get in so deep with our beliefs we forget where we end and the belief begins.

My beliefs in life dramatically changed when I realized this idea. The moment I wasn't able to give someone a scenario to scrutinize my beliefs, I realized I was only open to folks who were already on my side. It was never about the belief, many of the beliefs I held were handed down to me; I never owned them to begin with, but I did feel threatened by anyone who didn't share them because I simply began to believe that they were a part of me.

I realized how closed minded I had become, and how little I was learning. So I let them go. I embraced *I-don't-know-ism* and everyone I met was now a potential teacher and adventure.

People marry their beliefs and cannot fathom a life where they could believe anything to the contrary. They've closed doors, and take it personal when you say anything that doesn't align with their view. I don't blame them; who doesn't enjoy being agreed with and validated. Strong beliefs can serve as comfort zones, which although are a familiar feeling are no more than a graveyard for personal growth.

This chapter isn't for everyone, it's for the folks who are open to it. I'm writing this because I know there are individuals that want to divorce and unlearn some of the things that were poured into their minds at a very young age, but are afraid of the world after; don't be. The wisest ones are the ones that acknowledge how little they actually know.

I would love for you to write down the beliefs you value, and ask yourself where they came from. Then ask yourself if you can imagine life divorced from those beliefs. That version of me existed when I started this Humble The Poet journey. I was then blessed with opportunities of travel and meeting folks who were caring enough to f*ck with my beliefs until I realized I was just living off hand-me-down ideas, very few which agreed with my unique being.

You are not your beliefs.

Don't take offense if someone doesn't hold the same beliefs as you, and don't think it's beneficial to impose your beliefs on others. Be wary of the beliefs you hold that you cannot conceive of letting go.

We'd all be better off to continually reevaluate our relationships with our beliefs; they may be invisible anchors to an adventure of life long learning.

This may not be the most popular chapter in the book and I'm OK with that. I'm grateful that people don't see things the way I do, it's my opportunity to leave my comfort zones and grow.

You are not your beliefs.

36 ALLOW YOUR HEART SOME CHARACTER

The scratches and bruises add character. They give your heart a better look and feel.

It's can be a tough time. I'm lying, it WILL be a tough time, but so what, it should be so you'll come out of it a better person (or jaded).

Nature tends to dictate a balance, things work themselves out at pace not convenient to the entitled-self-indulged-ADD-gimme-gimme-gimme generation we belong to, but the balance and healing will come nonetheless.

Don't avoid the potential of a broken heart, you have the necessary tools to survive and blossom from it. Don't stay in a situation your heart left a long time ago.

Don't avoid the potential of a broken heart, you have the necessary tools to survive and blossom from it.

37 THE MORE WE LET GO, THE MORE WE GAIN

Sometimes happiness doesn't need to be achieved, we just have to make room for it. Our minds can be full of anxiety, regret, resentment, and worry that there's no room for the smiles.

Some people believe that what's happening to them determines their happiness, but the reality is, how they deal with those things determines how they feel.

Miserable thoughts may also be familiar, and familiarity can be a reason we hold to things much longer than their expiry date.

Let your yesterdays go, there will be a point where some of that pain will make sense, and some of it never will. We have this need to make sense of things, but it's at the expense of our ability to enjoy our NOW moments.

Leave the past where it belongs, the lessons will find you; focus on improving the way you feel now, it's all you have.

Some people believe that
what's happening to them
determines their happiness,
but the reality is, how
they deal with those things
determines how they feel.

38 HEARTBREAKS ARE ESSENTIAL

Intense pain can come from being jerked up out of a situation you so dearly valued, and being thrown into a world that feels so cold and unknown. You feel worthless, alone, and scared. Everything you knew, everything you wanted, and everything you understood, gone so swiftly.

I've had my heart broken, once or twice, or three or four times... I've lost count. Initially I thought, "Survive it once, it won't be so bad the second time." What I failed to realize is that the heart doesn't break the same way twice. Whatever got you the first time probably won't get you the second. Instead, something new, and more intense comes along to knock you over.

I've had my heart broken by friends, business partners, and girls (more than I care to admit), but I'm fortunate to have never experienced heartbreak at the hands of my family. Some of you reading this have. Betrayal sucks, and I'm sorry if reading this is reopening old wounds; as I said though, it's essential.

A broken heart is an injury on the inside, and with any injury, there's only so much you can do. You're mostly at the mercy of time. Time heals all, time reveals all, and it doesn't work on your schedule. During this time, life feels intense, difficult to bear, and sometimes even hopeless.

I just want to share some things I realized during that difficult time. None of this is easy, but it's good to keep in mind while time takes its course. Most of these ideas only gain relevance when you go through heartbreak, and it's these realizations that make me grateful for going through the experience.

- Your heart is an organ, and it's not broken, but the stress you're going through (combined with a lack of sleep and poor life choices) can seriously harm your health. Make healthy decisions. Drinking may appear to numb the pain, but it's really a depressant, a dangerous addiction and dependence can develop. My mother lost a brother to alcohol after his divorce. Alcohol and heartbreak don't mix.

- Even if you were dumped or cheated on (or worse), realize that relationships come to an end because of mismatches in compatibility and priorities. Never mistake incompatibility for your personal worth. If someone dumped you, it's because there wasn't a fit or you weren't taking them where they think they need to be. Even if they tell you "you're worthless," you're not. Even if you feel worthless, you're not. Your personal worth is determined by YOU. Never allow it to be dictated by another. If you can't love yourself, you have no business seeking love from others.
- To be betrayed means someone didn't live up to their end of the bargain. That bargain may have been assumed or explicit. Either way, promises are broken everyday, ignoring this fact is the reason the broken promise stings so much. Expectations are the key ingredient to disappointment; the less you expect from others, the less they can let you down.
- As much as your mind may say differently, all you have is NOW. Yesterday doesn't exist, the future can only be assumed. NOW is all you have, and it's what you need to focus on. We feel scared and confused when our plans are derailed. The truth is that uncertainty is the most realistic depiction of your future, get used to it. Change is not the enemy; it's the only consistency in your life. Focus on adapting.
- Happiness isn't what happens to you, it's how you deal with it. Again, this is easier said than done, but you're better off to even try to gain some control on deciding your emotions. We all have plenty to celebrate in our life. You can focus what you have or what you lost, but that focus is a choice, and the emotions that come with that focus are the consequence of the choice you make.
- Unhappiness is when the picture in your head doesn't match

the picture of your life. When you were a kid and wanted that toy, and mom said, "No," then dragged you out the store, you were heart broken. Maybe even so mad you didn't speak to her for a while, but you got over it. As you grow, your experiences will just be amplified versions of that story: you're not getting what you want. Realize that some things are in your control, and some are not. You need to meditate on what you can and cannot remedy. The things you can't, work to move on from them.

- Comparison is the thief of joy. Who gives a f*ck how many of your friends are in relationships.
- Finally... realize that everything you go through in life is temporary, including your life as a whole. In the grand scheme of things, you'll look back at these events and realize how little they matter. Harming yourself, or worse, can lead to PERMANENT problems. To be helpless is to feel like you're drowning, and the pain is deep, sickening, and it feels like there's no end in sight. PLEASE REMEMBER: with any problem you've had in your life history, time will help you adapt to the change and move forward. If the stress and pain is too much to deal with, seek PROFESSIONAL help. Your loved ones may have the best intentions, but they may not have the skill set to help you through what you're going through. Emotions are related to chemicals in your brain, we're all unique in our composition; it's OK if you need to seek additional support to get over what you're going through. I love you for the simple fact that you take the time to read my thoughts, so please remember that you're not alone, and you don't have to go through it alone. There are people who want to help and who know how to help.

The butterfly has to struggle in the cocoon to break out. If you were to help it by cutting the cocoon open, it wouldn't develop the necessary muscles to fly. Its beauty comes from its struggles and so does yours. Heartbreak, like any other struggle, is essential for your growth.

Heartbreak, like any other struggle, is essential for your growth.

30 ANOTHER LESSON FROM 50 CENT

"...pray or worry -- don't do both" - 50 Cent

Regardless of your spiritual inclinations, this quote hits a chord. It comes down to our need for control; our need to understand and make sense of things; and our need to NEED. Our minds are dramatically more complex than other life forms, but that's not necessarily always a good thing.

We internalize things more and manufacture suffering. No animals are worried about what time it is, or being late, or even running out of time. Animals only experience fear in the present, and that fear is what they use to get out of danger. Our fears plant seeds in our brain to grow into things we have yet to experience or finished experiencing a long time ago. For reasons like this, we've done wonders in the field of suffering.

There isn't a pill for this.

Worry exists in the future, and like depression of the past, it can spiral out of control very quickly. The anxiety that comes with worry and depression is no longer mental or physical, and will f*ck you up. A worry, one that is unaddressed, can chip away at your life. Respecting the nature of things isn't a 'Zen-Buddha-be-one-with-nature' mentality.

It simply encourages one to respect the way things are setup, and their nature, and our relationship to them. Some sh*t you can change and some sh*t is still beyond you; maneuver accordingly.

Don't get me wrong, although it feels like sh*t sometimes worrying comes in handy; nothing is absolute. I'm also sure it's part of our general mental makeup, so at best we can only reduce the frequency of our worries. A reduction in worry is still a step up in our quality of life.

It's an exercise of letting go. When we remember that we have limited resources (internally and externally), only then can we use them with an enhanced wisdom. Many situations and people that occupy our minds may no longer warrant such attention when it comes to the grand scheme of things. The end game is death, and you can see that as depressing or liberating.

Only you know if your worrying is warranted; it's an expense you primarily pay.

"Worry does not empty tomorrow of its sorrow, it empties today of its strength." — Corrie ten Boom

"Worry does not empty tomorrow of its sorrow, it empties today of its strength."

40 PEOPLE ARE EXPENSIVE

It's always wise to take inventory of the people in your life. It's irrelevant if they're family, friends, acquaintances, or colleagues. If they're being toxic, cut them off.

You don't know how much time you have on this planet so don't waste those limited moments with folks that don't deserve your company.

Never allow people that care little about you to have a grand impact on how you feel. Don't compromise yourself and make concessions to keep these types of people around; F*ck'em. Liberating yourself from them not only teaches you what to avoid in the future, but also positions you in a situation where you can now find folks that you actually vibe with.

You can't pay for a vibe. Chemistry is chemistry, and not everyone gets along as easily as they do with others. That's a reality of life you'll be better off working with, rather than pounding your head in impossible situations simply because you don't want to be alone.

Your time is limited, so please be picky about the people you spend it with...

41
SOMETIMES WE NEED TO SUFFER

I read about this couple that committed suicide. They ran a self-help motivational radio show called "The Pursuit of Happiness" which heavily promoted positive thinking. Though the motivation behind their suicide is unknown, the article used them as a segue to discuss the potential dangers of prescribing to that mindset.

I'm using that story as a segue because I just read about it, so now it's going to inspire my own reflections. I've been having my own struggles with staying positive (note the present tense) and it slowed down my productivity, creativity, and just my overall ability to be in the company of others.

It sometimes feels like when you think positive there's another voice that fires back immediately with a negative thought, and that voice feels a whole lot more familiar and sure of itself. That's not something you can deny away.

Finding something to appreciate and having a positive outlook is important, but becoming idealistic, and hoping for a fairy tale ending will require much more self-convincing, and will wear off quickly resulting in bitterness.

I guess I need to remind myself that emotions are all important, even the negative thoughts, and instead of trying to scream over them with pseudo-positive-mantras, I should be quiet, listen, and pay attention to what they're saying; then have a conversation.

People can make a lot of money promising to liberate you from suffering, but suffering is a key reason we evolve and improve our situation. It's not in our nature to be at peace, that's why first world problems exist. Once your basic needs are met, you make up a bunch of new ones to be sad about.

For better or worse, our feelings change with time. Change is the promise. We all fall into funks, and we should take a little solace to remember that we're not alone; we just think we are.

It's OK to have a bad day, stop assuming others don't just because you don't see it.

Also keep in mind, if we do the same things everyday we'll get the same result, so if your funk feels a bit longer than it should, switch up your game plan until you see the change.

Suffering is a key reason we evolve and improve our situation.

42 FALLING IN LOVE WITH LEARNING

As a teacher, it was always stressed that I didn't simply focus on filling the kids' heads with knowledge, but rather light a fire in them for the love of learning.

I love learning new sh*t. I'm excited at the idea of getting exposed to things I never knew existed. It's mind blowing how much there is to discover on this tiny speck in the universe. I also keep mindful of the things I think I already know. Once upon a time people knew the world was flat and the sun rotated around the earth. When I was a kid, we knew Pluto was a planet. Even the things we think are common knowledge and common sense are flipped on their head.

I'm not monogamous with those ideas. I don't identify myself by the things I believe, it's a fickle foundation to stand on. Rather I take pride in my commitment to unlearning and letting go of stale ideas that no longer agree with me.

You just need a conversation with yourself to see what you agree with. We all have gut feelings; I'd trust those, after all who has your best interest in mind more than you.

There are different types of education and even more ways for folks to learn. We all process information uniquely, if you figure out your preferred method, mix that with a topic you're inclined towards, you can have a lot of fun geeking out.

We're all geeks for something; cars, video games, Game of Thrones, Hip Hop, Star Trek, Star Wars, fashion, etc. Find the things you enjoy and immerse yourself in them. Find other folks who go bananas over the things you've never explored, and let them be your tour guide.

I know that sometimes new things can be frightening and uncomfortable, but that's the recipe for growth. Also, turning our brain on to be continually mining for opportunities to learn prepares us to deal with the not-so-pleasant-times in life. Failure becomes success the moment we learn from it.

...new things can be frightening and uncomfortable, but that's the recipe for growth.

43
LESS EXPECTATIONS LESS DISAPPOINTMENTS

We all have expectations and I would be a delusional-idealist to promote a life without them. Rather, we can, at the very least, use our disappointed moments to recognize the root of our expectations. Sometimes we may find that having such an expectation isn't wise, or realistic, or even necessary.

I still have expectations of people, professionally and personally, and both still tend to let me down. If the behavior is repeated into a pattern, it's on me to pay attention. I try my best never to play victim because there's no empowerment in feeling like one. Blame and power go hand in hand, so giving it away may not be the best choice.

When someone let's us down, we can take the time to figure out if we want to allow that to happen again. After all, the past is just that, the past. We can only focus on improving the choices of our present to hopefully have a better future.

I know some of you reading this have been deeply hurt by people. Within that pain are jewels of wisdom that can put you in a position not to repeat the same foibles. Our heart is very resilient, and it will survive even when someone steps all over it.

For my readers, who have taken a few extra laps around the sun, you know this too well. Things that feel like the end of our world rarely are. We can all be a bit over dramatic, and we need to realize we're harming no one else but ourselves.

The responsibilities involved with your heart, rely solely on you. Don't put yourself in positions for others to damage you, and if you do (which you will), learn from those mistakes, so they don't hopefully happen again.

Pay attention to actions over words, they'll always be more revealing.

I love you for reading this, but I have no intention of shielding you from the pain that life brings; it's essential. We learn best the hard way, unfortunately, but the next time you go through it, at the very least you may remember these words.

Blame and power go
hand in hand

FITTING IN IS A POINTLESS ACTIVITY

When it's your time to die it's going to be a solo activity, so don't let the choices you make while you're alive depend on the approval of others. When it's all said and done, they're not coming with you.

I write a lot about death, mainly because it's the most liberating idea that comes to my mind. Most of the things that bog our mind with worry are just manufactured by our imagination, and the reminder of death does well to belittle their importance. There is a grand scheme of things, and when you think of it, you realize not only should you not sweat the small stuff, but that it's ALL small stuff.

Every moment you receive is yours and yours alone. You choose to waste it away, lost in the past, or worried about your future, or you choose to enjoy it by allowing yourself to be present in it. The company you keep is also a choice of yours, and if the people you have around you don't appreciate you for the unique creation you are then move on. Life isn't long enough to win folks over nor is it ever worth the effort to seek approval from the judgmental.

Many of those in history that we celebrate now, did not receive the same accolades during their lifetime. Some of the thoughts and ideas they expressed may not have been the most comforting and convenient. Yet, well after they were gone, they became considered ahead of their time. I doubt many of those folks that accomplished great things did it solely for the accolades, or for our feeble approval years later. They had faith in what they were doing, and even if the world seemed against them, they pushed forward.

History is written with a bias, and folks are either uber-demonized or uber-glorified, both forgetting that people are not simple black and white beings. This serves well for our continual efforts to simplify the world, but does little for people who catch themselves in comparison. One of my favourite human beings is Malcolm X for the simple fact that he acknowledged and repented his own biases and closed mindedness when having new experiences in life. It's OK not to be perfect, no one before you ever was, and if anyone claims they were, it's probably a claim made after the fact.

We each have an awesome uniqueness within us, and we could probably use those individual traits to benefit others and ourselves. To discover those gems will require some internal treasure hunting so I recommend you start digging.

Digging inside doesn't require the approval of folks on the outside.

We each have an awesome
uniqueness within us, and we
could probably use those
individual traits to benefit
ourselves and others.

45 GHOSTBUSTERS

We're all haunted by ghosts; the ghosts of our past. The intense regret that comes from the mistakes we're bound to make on this journey of life. The haunting is optional though, as the past isn't real, neither are ghosts, unless we allow them to be.

On a daily basis, I, like everyone else, is plagued with the coulda-woulda-shouldas of life. I catch myself wishing I made better decisions in certain situations. I also wish I could take back things I've done and said to people that are no longer in my life. The reality is I simply can't. Regret is a pointless practice, and an expensive one at that.

The only thing in our possession is the present, like right NOW; tomorrow isn't promised; and yesterday never will be again. What's done is done. It'd be too idealistic to assume we can live free of our past, as we are a product of it, but we can use those experiences to extract lessons that will benefit our present, and subsequent future.

Life is a painting, comprised of brushstrokes. Every moment is a brushstroke, and there's very little you can do once the paint is on the canvas. The skill that we can all develop (slowly) is to filter out the best from each moment, and allow the rest to disappear, as it should.

Live in the moment; it's cliché, but it's true. These moments are gifts squandered while we focus on the ones that have already past, or the ones we hope to come in the future. We're happiest when we're in the moment, it's probably why folks have sex, gamble, drive their cars really fast, meditate, or do any other activity that dissolves a wandering mind.

The fact remains that the past no longer exists, and if we dedicate our limited presence towards pondering it with no benefit to our nows and tomorrows then we're sabotaging ourselves.

Letting go of the past is a scary, but liberating process (not claiming it's easy, nothing worthwhile ever is, but if that's what you were thinking you me another $5).

Free yourself from your past. The present is a gift, and you deserve to enjoy it.

These moments are gifts
squandered while we focus
on the ones that have already
past, or the ones we hope
to come in the future.

46 YOU CAN'T SAVE'EM ALL

What you'll notice is, the ones that make the most forward progress in life are the ones that are the most open to change. Many folks tell you their problems simply to vent and don't really care for any constructive solutions, as those constructive solutions may require them to leave their beloved comfort zones.

We're only equipped with so much time and energy, and it can get expensive if we spend that frivolously on folks who have no intention outside of sucking us dry. People love attention, and sometimes the only way they think they can get it is through tugging on the strings of our hearts.

In no way am I advocating we all become self-indulged islands of apathy (though it wouldn't hurt to admit that there are elements of that in us). I'm simply saying to be mindful of people who may be exploiting your kindness for purposes outside of bettering themselves.

We ALL have our own struggles; personally I don't want to weigh down the people I love with my problems. I ask for assistance, but also try to bring value to the people around me. Personally I prefer to pick peoples brains over meals and learn that way. I've also noticed that when many folks look for advice, they've already made up their mind, and are merely looking for some affirmation and validation for that decision.

Trust your gut; there isn't anyone else out there more qualified to deal with you than yourself. When folks come to you for help, be mindful of their intention, they may not be evident at first, but they will be very soon. Some folks will appreciate you teaching them to fish, while others will continue come back for another hand out.

Empathy can be exploited, and in turn that can turn us off to helping others in the future, which would be a shame. Put folks in a position to help themselves, everyone wins in that situation, and that support can be paid forward.

...when many folks look for advice, they've already made up their mind, and are merely looking for some affirmation and validation for that decision.

47 IT HURTS TO CARE SOMETIMES

Especially when that level of caring and attention aren't reciprocated. We feel used, or under appreciated. Some of us cling to hope that things will get better, but really it most likely won't. The relationship that needs the most work in this situation is the one we have with reality. The writing tends to be on the wall with the people we surround ourselves with; sometimes we just don't want to read it.

There are people who keep me around because they can be themselves around me, and I don't take advantage of that. I aim to keep folks of that caliber around me as well.

There have been plenty who have wronged me by exploiting my kind actions, but I'm not going to grow cold because of that. I like caring, I like giving, and I'll continue to work towards being around the folks who deserve that.

You already know if someone isn't worth your love, so why you keeping them around?

Don't care less, just be wiser about who you care for; some folks deserve more than you can give; others deserve less than they're getting.

You already know if someone isn't worth your love, so why you keeping them around?

48 WHICH EMOTIONS ARE YOU FEEDING?

Stuff happens in our lives, emotions can overwhelm us, and sometimes it's just not easy to appreciate the sunshine, or the air in our lungs, or anything else for that matter.

We all feel it; the heavy emotions that we think no one else understands. The pain that wears a half-ass smile and has mastered the art of saying, "I'm fine," which is short for, "Leave me alone, you wouldn't understand if I tried to explain it, and you probably wouldn't care either."

Accepting fear, confusion, anxiety, and whatever other unpleasantness simply means to understand it's a part of us, no different than a toenail or nose hair. The most extraordinary people feel those emotions too; they just choose not to feed them.

You can feed your emotions, and regardless of how you're feeling at the moment, you have some control in determining the direction of the spiral to follow. These emotions feed off you, whether it's happiness or depression, they will feed off your energy until you're consumed with them. Which emotions do you want to be consumed with?

People always ask me, "Why do I feel like this; why does this happen; why do other people say…," and the answer is I don't know why most things happen; I don't really care. Instead, I make the effort to focus on what I want to happen and what I need to do to get there.

Appreciation and gratitude makes great food for the belly of your happiness; worry and regret do wonders to chub up your depression. Decide which emotions you want to feed.

These emotions feed off you, whether it's happiness or depression, they will feed off your energy until you're consumed with them. Which one do you want to be consumed with?

49 YOU CAN'T PROTECT YOUR BUBBLE

As life progresses, the oversold romance and idealism starts to wither away. The good guys don't always win; telling the truth isn't always the best policy; and you realize that no one promised the world would be fair.

The issues aren't these realities; they're not even the cause of our misery. The issues are the relationships we hold with these realities, and how unhealthy they can become.

The happy endings only exist in the movies and fables, and it doesn't bother me to understand this, it liberates me from that expectation. We don't need to be in these bubbles; they do nothing for us, but set us up for a pop. The longer it takes, the higher we've floated, the harder the fall.

The fear of uncomfortable ideas, and uncomfortable situations, and uncomfortable places robs us of the amazing potential we all have.

When you start to admit your fears, you'll realize how much of this world is governed by fear. 15,000 years of recorded human history, and you'll see fear from day one. We all feel fear, that's OK, my only beef is the ignorant bubbles we build to protect ourselves from the things we fear.

The truth is the pin that bursts those bubbles. Those truths that remind us that politicians have NEVER been trustworthy; people have always been self-indulged creatures of habit and prejudice; and that no matter how high we try to put ourselves on a pedestal, the ugliest things that have ever occurred on this planet have come from our hands.

We are Hitler; we are Obama; we are Osama; we are Gangis Khan. We are also Steve Jobs, Baba Nanak, Bruce Lee, Bob Marley, and Rumi.

We are everything we hate about this world, and we are everything we love about it, and the biggest problem is we'll never see the WE, only the you and me. The brief moments in life when the ego melts, beautiful things happen, but the brief moments are just that, brief.

As brief as they are, I think they're worth sticking around for. Let those bubbles pop, the fresh air tastes beautiful.

The fear of uncomfortable
ideas, and uncomfortable
situations, and uncomfortable
places robs us of the amazing
potential we all have.

50 YOU HAVE TO DO WHAT'S BEST FOR YOU

There's a difference between wanting what's best, and knowing what's best. Many people in our lives want what's best for us. Their intentions may be pure, but that doesn't mean they understand us enough to know what would really be in our best interest.

Even with ourselves, with VIP access to our inner most thoughts and desires, we can easily get the signals crossed as to what's best for us. There can sometimes be this need to give off an impression to the outward world, or live up to societal expectations, even if those choices push us away from what our inning core wants.

It's ironic that some of the most celebrated individuals are celebrated for just that, not molding themselves to the world, but rather attempting to mold the world to themselves. I was raised in a Sikh household with numerous stories of civil disobedience, and challenges to the authority, but when it came to my life it was, "Do as your told."

I'm not here to advocate a life of disobedience to your family, or society, or whoever. I'm here to say that life isn't one size fits all. What's good for them may not be good for you. Society seems to have a formula for the best way to exist, but if that formula doesn't agree with yourself, then grab a pen, and make some revisions.

Please understand though, that the more freedom you claim, the more weight you hold, and responsibilities you'll have. People walk the easy beaten path because, after all, it's easy. The idea of challenges in life is not everyone's cup of tea; but I can promise you, greatness wouldn't feel great if it came easy.

No one knows you better than yourself, and your yardstick for success should be based on, and measured, by yourself, not others. Don't play the game that others play, where they build a shell of a life just for display purposes. Have a life of substance that you want, even if that isn't what others feel is best for you.

No one else can live this life for you.

Society seems to have a formula for the best way to exist, but if that formula doesn't agree with yourself, then grab a pen, and make some revisions.

51 THE RELIGION OF 'WANT'

Do we even know the difference between want and need anymore? What we wanted last year, doesn't seem to be enough this year, or the next. What stimulated us yesterday is an afterthought today. The religion (and yes it's a religion) where believing that holding things will make us happy is a very expensive lifestyle.

When I say expensive, I don't just mean on your wallet. Financial stresses wiggle their way into other aspects of our lives, and can do a number on the relationships we have with others.

Consumer culture isn't set up for your benefit, it's set up to suck you dry. An abundance of "Fight Club" quotes comes to mind, and they all hold true:
"We buy things we don't need, to impress people we don't like."

We have this inclination to plant our flag into things to identify ourselves, our style, our possessions, and our beliefs. The issue with this arises when we forget that these disposable items create a disposable identity.

Depending on your age, and stage in life, this chapter will ring true a bit more. Some of you are spending your part-time job money on the finer things in life, while others are working 60 hours a week just to keep your lips above the water. I'm not here to judge your lifestyle decisions; I'm here to ask you to think about them.

"The things you own end up owning you." - Tyler Durden

I promise you, the best things in life aren't things at all. Instead, find the smiles from within and share them on the outside.

I promise you, the best things
in life aren't things at all.

52

DON'T LET SOMEONE ELSE WRITE YOUR STORY

It's your story, don't let someone else hold the pen.

Sometimes I make decisions and ask myself, "Is this the right thing to do? I don't know anyone else doing that? Am I normal?"

There's no such thing as normal. You are who you are. What makes you interesting are the unique things you say, do, and think. All those unique actions make up your unique story. All those unique twists and turns in your story make it worth reading.

Some folks search for happiness making money, others building bridges, others finding love, others by saying mean things on Youtube It doesn't matter if they ever find it, as long as they're choosing their own journey.

There's no right or wrong lifestyle if it's the lifestyle that makes you feel the most alive. You've been afforded very limited time on this planet; use that time wisely. Wisely for some may not be wisely for others, and that's OK.

Once you determine and create your purpose, you may even find multiple roads to take you to that same spot. Happiness is a mindstate, I can find it while I'm on stage, and when I'm nose to nose with my niece, and those are the stories worth living, worth telling, and worth remembering because each of those opportunities rejuvenates our smile.

I don't have to write music to enjoy my passion, I just have to write. It can be a two-liner, paragraph, full essay, or even a book. Sometimes I don't even have to write, as I find the same joy in reading the writings of other awesome writers. I realized on my journey that I love creativity, so now any path that brings me closer to creativity is a path I'm open to.

Simplify your loves and explore all the routes that take you there. That's what's going to make for an awesome story. Don't bind yourself by the expectations of others; it's not their story to write.

You've been afforded very limited time on this planet; use that time wisely, and wisely for some may not be wisely for others, and that's OK.

53 DEPENDING ON LUCK IS FOR SUCKERS

The hardest working people tend to be the luckiest. They stay prepared and seek opportunities to capitalize off, in order to move forward. The concept of random luck, like lottery tickets, is reserved for the entitled and inactive (i.e. lazy folks).

Random sh*t will always happen, that's a given. The only way to remedy hard luck is with hard work. The curve balls that life throws you are only going to be an issue if you haven't been practicing your swing.

I'm a huge proponent of the alchemy concept. That's the idea that we can turn anything into a golden opportunity. One of the first things required is to be dramatically less judgmental. We tend to evaluate things simplistically like, "Is this what I wanted?" "No" = Bad, "Yes" = Good. This logic is flawed.

All of us have experienced things we wanted and later regretted; and plenty of us have gone through what we thought was a horrible situation, only to realize it was a defining moment in our life.

Instead of jumping the gun, we should calm down, take a deep breath and examine our situations thoroughly. Opportunities exist everywhere; they're not in plain sight. If they were easy to find, there wouldn't be much benefit to finding them. Start digging and asking yourself, "How can I turn this sh*t to sugar," you'll have to be creative, but the ideas that come from within will astonish you.

There are a million stories of folks who took the momentum of some severe incident, and used it for their benefit. There is so much beauty that can only find its inspiration amongst the ugly of the world. It just requires an open mind that is willing to shed biases and allow itself to roam around seeing the problems from all angles.

Stop looking at things simplistically; there is no good and bad, and luck is simply the blend of opportunity and preparation. Many of my counterparts have been afforded the same opportunities as me, but weren't prepared, and that's why they're not in my spot (ask them though, and they'll say I'm lucky).

Sikhi has a concept of *tyar bar tyar* meaning "always be prepared."

Figure out what you want, and prepare for it. Have faith in your power of alchemy to turn every opportunity to gold.

We tend to evaluate things
simplistically like,
"Is this what I wanted?"
"No" = Bad, "Yes" = Good.
This logic is flawed.

54 I MET THIS GIRL ONCE...

Artist type... she could draw and had a creative mind. She never watched TV, back then that was cool, and most importantly she had been crushing on me for a few years. Things moved quickly, like any guy I wasn't complaining. We probably got much closer physically before we did emotionally, again, I wasn't complaining.

Then one night she revealed that as a child, her grandfather would do inappropriate things to her, and that although she tried to tell her parents, it fell on deaf ears. She told me how she still trembled when she sees him, and he conducts himself hoping she was too young to remember.

I was a lot younger then and had no idea how to respond to that. At that point in my bubble-boy life, I didn't know things like that really happened, let alone at the hands of a Punjabi grandpa. I don't remember how I reacted, I only know it never came up again.

I met another girl once...

She wasn't Punjabi, but close enough. This situation was very exciting, secret rendezvous, very superficial, straight to business. After a few weeks, there was a minor argument, and when I went to use the bathroom, she disappeared. I ran around the area to find her trying to hitch a cab. She was hysterical. I calmed her down, and in my typical insensitive manner asked her why she freaked out so quickly. Turns out she had issues with conflict, mostly stemming from the fact that she was sexually abused by her grandfather, and any conflict or betrayal just stabbed her and threw her into panic mode. This time around I hugged her as tight as I could and let her know this isn't the case.

I could also tell you about my homeboy and what his daddy did to him growing up, or the young girl I went to Gurmat Camp with at the Gurdwara and what a Baba tried to do to her.

The stories I'm sharing are stories that aren't being shared. Similar to the stories of girls in Delhi that NEVER report abuse or the fact that a girl in South Africa has a better chance of being raped than learning to read.

Death penalties, extended prison terms, or whatever other reactions to quell the protesting public, cannot immediately reverse generations upon generations of female subordination. All individuals SHOULD be able to wear whatever and travel wherever they please without the fear of attack, but that's idealistic, and ignores the harsh elements of the creature known as human.

The reality is that the only person we can trust is ourselves, and we need to create a situation of self-sufficiency and depend on no legal apparatus or organization to protect us from individuals looking to violate us. The idea that we're civilized creatures will only further our dependency on the systems that can do very little to protect us. Please put yourself in a position to protect yourself and those around you.

Change is most effective on a local level, even more effective in the home. I hope when you read your flooded social media timelines with stories of shootings, rape victims succumbing to their injuries, or committing suicide, you are motivated to take preventative measures for yourself and those around you.

With children, cultivate a culture where secrets are forbidden. NO SECRETS, PERIOD. Also, my nephew won't open the door or get in a car with me unless his mother says it's OK first. That doesn't bother me, it's a small price to know that his trust cannot be exploited to harm him.

The blame game is a displacement of responsibility and should be left to the idiotic politicians, media, and online 'slactivists'. Statistics show this is happening to someone you may know or love right now. Take whatever steps you see fit to ensure we're not reading about their unhappy ending in the future. Use the memory of these young girls and boys to ensure others still have a future.

I hope none of you reading can relate to these stories, but then I'd be the disillusioned idealist. We can't erase your past, but you have the power to make a better future.

The blame game is a
displacement of responsibility,
and should be left to the
idiotic politicians, media,
and online 'slactivists'

55 DON'T KNOW YOURSELF, CAN'T BE YOURSELF

Our biggest enemy in the pursuit of getting to know ourselves is ourselves.

We have a need for attention, or validation rather. We send signals out, and really hope to get them back. If you tell a joke, and nobody laughs, what are the chances of you telling it again? If everyone laughs milk out of their noses, what are the chances you'll wiggle it into a conversation in front of a new crowd? People do it all the time; comedians do it for a living.

Needing attention and observing what works and what doesn't, fulfills that need, paints us a new picture of ourselves, which over time distances ourselves from who we really are. We tend to not express ourselves, but rather express what works, and what makes us stand out or fit in. Facebook has done a wonderful job quantifying this with the ever so precious LIKE button.

I have people that love me dearly and they read some of the unflattering comments on my wall. They tell me that they don't know how I can put up with it. The truth is, I couldn't in the beginning. When I started this in 2008, I received nothing but love, I was the underdog, everyone was rooting for my success. Fast forward a few years, there's a section in my stadium dedicated to finding a reason to criticize. At first I would tell myself things like, "Oh they're just haters, they're jealous, they don't know what they're saying," but the comments didn't really start to bounce off until I divorced the need to hear the GOOD stuff as well.

The positive comments are just as valid and invalid as the negative ones. They are opinions expressed by people I don't know. It's impossible to sit back enjoy all the great things people say to me, then close the door to not-so-great. Instead I had to learn to stop defining myself and allowing myself to be affected by any opinion, positive or negative (it's an ongoing process).

I CAN'T learn about myself by focusing on HOW others see me, but I can learn by focusing on WHY I care. I'd be lying if I said I didn't care. We all care, but I do notice we tend to care a lot less as we get older. I'm not sure if that's because we've spent enough time with ourselves to develop a better relationship with who we are, or we're just too old and tired of trying to keep up.

Just like any other substance, validation and attention can become things we depend on. Think about relationships, and the amount of worth placed on having others to love, others to talk to, or others to simply be around. I've been dumped by girls, and my self-worth has gone down the drain. The fear of rejection keeps many of us from doing what we want because we allow these events to count on our scoreboard of self-worth.

The fear of loneliness comes into play as well. I think SOME folks don't enjoy being alone because they don't enjoy their own company. Maybe it's because they don't feel they live up to their own expectations or because it's as awkward as being stuck in a room with a stranger. A lot of the relationships we have are based on how the other person makes us feel about ourselves, and that only heightens the sense of loss at their departure. Leaders need followers to be leaders.

Humble The Poet needs an audience to be a public figure. The dependency is there, but the compromises made to maintain the relationships are what's important.

I'm not sharing this to put people down for having that need; we're all in it together. Media does a great job of making us feel inferior to sell us something that'll improve that situation. Although the fear is real, the consequences are not; the fear is simply being exploited. In reality, the people we admire most, have (or project) a confidence we want, and the most celebrated of them are the ones that are so unique you couldn't copy them if you tried. You can't buy confidence, it has to be developed, and like a language, it's going to take time.

That uniqueness comes from a lot of soul searching and most of that is through conversations with yourself when you're alone. Some call this meditation, some call it *Me* time, and others call it peace and solitude.

As someone who relies on attention to make a living, I can promise that even if the lights and cameras get brighter and fancier, happiness won't follow. The more we paint ourselves based on how others see us, the stronger our reputation is formed. That reputation is a prison, and we'll only start freeing ourselves, when we start being ourselves. In addition, encourage others to be themselves and validate their unique qualities.

You can only start being yourself when you start to get to know yourself. So turn off the distractions, sit down, and have a conversation with the most important person in your life... YOU.

I CAN'T learn about myself by focusing on HOW others see me, but I can learn by focusing on WHY I care.

56

OH MAN, HOW SCARY IT IS TO ASK FOR HELP

I remember the times in my life when I f*cked up on a major scale and was just too scared and embarrassed to admit it. I didn't want to ask for help to remedy my situations because I didn't want people to think less of me.

Now, I wouldn't speak to someone who judged me enough to think less of me.

I'm a human being. You're a human being (or some sort of odd literate primate). We are bound to mess up and make mistakes. Generally the largest casualty is our pride.

Bruised egos are miniscule, but have the ability to feel amplified beforehand. It's part of the fear we manufacture in our minds to avoid becoming uncomfortable.

My ego has done much harm in my journey through life and being Humble The Poet. I almost let it get in the way of some of the greatest experiences and people I could have ever come across.

Most of the things that have held me back are associated with my pride or what I feel others may think of me. Everyday I work to shed that pointless concern. It's uncomfortable, but that's how I know I'm in a position to grow.

Sikh philosophy uses a great analogy of truth being a door, the size of a mustard seed, while our pride is comparable to an elephant. We need to shed it before we can move forward.

I can't say it's possible to be free of all pride, as that's too absolute for my reality, but I can attest that the more you let go, the more free you'll feel.

A lot of times, that *letting go* can come in the form of reaching out to others.

I can attest that the more you let go, the more free you'll feel.

57 ARE YOU HAPPY?

There are a lot of folks who don't feel like life is going the way they want it to go.

When that picture in your head doesn't match the picture in front of you, the result for many is unhappiness.

That picture could be of the world as a whole, or your personal life, or the expectation that there's going to be a twist at the end of the film, "ZeroDarkThirty" (Spoiler Alert: Osama dies). The constant comparison of what's in our head to what's in front of our face does a lot to determine our mood.

Though what we forget is that often times what's in our heads hasn't ever existed for us or anyone else. As a rapper, there's a common practice of creating an image that doesn't exist. A lot of these artists create that image using material goods and manufactured fun in music videos.

None of us want to admit that we're suckers of media manipulation; it's either that or the fairy tales. There hasn't been an instance of world peace in human history, nor has there been a chunk of time where human exploitation wasn't present. Utopias do exist in the movies, where the good king regains his throne and rules fairly over the land (how the f*ck can one dude ruling over many people ever be described as fair?).

Having expectations in general is a great way to secure some unhappiness and disappointment in life. Having UNREALISTIC expectations just magnifies the delusion and frustration.

"Hey man, you must be swimming in women." "Boy, I wish I had your life, sleep in all day, write a few poems, travel the world." "Man, you're so famous, life must be awesome."

I haven't really shot any music videos depicting such a lifestyle, but people project these things upon me, not because they believe it of me, but more so they want and need to believe that this lifestyle can exist. None of my wealthy friends sleep in, the only ones I know that do are unemployed.

That may come from watching too much Entourage, Sex in the City, or whatever other shows folks escape to after a long day. Personally, I think I do have an awesome life, not for any of the aforementioned assumptions (double big word bonus), but rather because I'm actively searching for reasons to be happy and grateful in my present existence and I'm continually divorcing my feelings from my circumstances.

Call it stoicism, pessimism, or realism, I call it just living and learning. Detachment is stressed in Sikh philosophy. Attachment is identified as a larger thief of contentment than anger, greed, or lust. We're such socialized creatures we don't even realize how attached we are to the things that were taught to us growing up. Many of them are inaccurate, irrelevant, or simply redundant to the world we live in, and the unique individuals we are.

Only you know the lies you still cling to. Figure out where they came from, and try letting them go. Then think about it again:

Are you Happy?

Having expectations in general
is a great way to secure some
unhappiness and disappointment
in life. Having UNREALISTIC
expectations just magnifies
the delusion and frustration.

58 REGRETS ARE STUPID

The past doesn't exist anymore, and it never will ever again. Allowing your decisions from this non-existent period of time to cause you pain is counter-productive to the time you have in the present.

We've all f*cked up and made some bone-headed moves. We re-watch the footage over and over and over again wishing we could Marty McFly our way back to that very moment so we can change things for the better. The flaw in this, beyond the fact that time travel is yet to exist, is that there's no guarantee that altering the past would have made for a better present.

As non-existent as the past is, the future is unsure. Cause and effect are things we wish we could simplify, but we really can't. You don't know how things would have been different so stop wasting calories worrying about it. What you can be sure about is your present state, and that this very moment is your opportunity to make the life you want to have.

We are a sum of our experiences, including the not-so-proud moments we all go through. People make mistakes, but are given the option to grow from them. Not only should you not allow your past to be held against you, it's very bone-headed to hold other's past against them.

The coulda-woulda-shouldas of life are a waste of time, for the simple fact that focusing on them will yield nothing. You end up wasting the time you have now; suffering for a time you've already left behind.

173

Most regrets folks tend to have, near the end of life, are things they didn't do. So focus on the life you want, and realize that, although regret is a stupid thing to have, allowing fear to prevent you from living the life you want is just as, if not more, stupid. It's also a guarantee for regret in the future. Don't fear the pain of work; it's nothing in comparison to the pain of regret.

Anything you've messed up in the past can be chalked up to a life lesson and experience. Success is a horrible teacher, so rely on the missteps and failures to guide you on this adventure of life.

And f*ck all the I–told-you-so folks in your life. These people are despicable and use your misfortunes as opportunities to stroke their own feeble egos. Nothing good comes from pointless opinions after the fact, so tell these people to f*ck off (or say something a with a bit more tact).

You are a piece of art in progress, constantly improving everyday. Seek experiences in the world, make mistakes, and allow them to shape the person you are. Celebrate that person you're becoming; you're one in 100 billion humans to have ever existed. Every scar, nook, cranny, mistake, achievement, and tear makes up your unique composition.

Don't waste this amazing human experience on a time and place you're never going to revisit. Be present, move forward, and let go of everything else.

You end up wasting the time
you have now; suffering for a
time you've already left behind.

59 NOBODY FITS IN

What the f*ck are folks trying to fit into anyways? Whose specific approval are you looking for? Society is not a person, it doesn't have a personality, and it can't make judgments.

From your genetic code up to your favorite flavor of ice cream, you are different. Those distinctions about you are what make you who you are. I'm not going to call you special because that's corny. I can say you have the ability to take your unique attributes and celebrate them in a way that will encourage other people to do the same.

People are attracted to confidence, that's it. Confidence comes from a comfort in your own skin. I know plenty of folks who've been given a genetic makeup that is very pleasing to the eye, and even they have insecurities they battle with on a daily basis.

Pay attention to the people you keep around you. They may attempt to project their insecurities onto you so they don't feel like the only ones.

I had friends in my circle that only functioned on some ego trip, telling me I shouldn't be too available to fans and I need some mystique on my brand. For a long second I believed them, and then common sense gave me a roundhouse kick to the nose, reminding me that the people who take the time to check out my work mean a hell of a lot more than the ones looking to capitalize off of it.

Be yourself and believe in yourself. Confidence isn't a light switch; it's a foundation you build. Work hard at something and take pride in the accomplishments. Don't act like you're better than anyone and don't act like anyone is better than you.

Relying on people and possessions to improve how you feel about yourself is fickle. It'll last only as long as the things you've acquired stay validating, which won't be long. Focus on the inside and develop your qualities that no one can take from you.

For me, those things are my ability to love and tell the truth, what's yours?

Confidence isn't a light switch;
it's a foundation you build

60 ALL MY MOTHERS

Mama Earth, Mama Toronto, Mama Poet and My Sisters.

For every mother that birthed us, raised us, taught us, punished us, protected us, educated us, and loved us like no one else could... we love you.

To the beautiful people in our lives that may not have been afforded the luxury of having their biological mother around, may the rest of us spread the abundance of love we have their way.

There's nothing we can do to give a mother a day off. Once she's assumed that role, it's a lifelong position that fills her entire being with perpetual concern for those she created. There's no off switch, which for the rest of us is a blessing.

For every mother that birthed
us, raised us, taught us,
punished us, protected us,
educated us, and loved us
like no one else could...

61

ONLY BORING PEOPLE GET BORED

Though I'm not immune to clutches of procrastination, there's never an absence of things to do. The idea of boredom is a luxury, and is generally a byproduct of leisure time.

An easy boredom killer is trying something new (I know, pretty revolutionary). You don't know if you'll enjoy something unless you try it, and you can only try it if you're open to it. Being open to trying new things, though sometimes daunting, is the best way to broaden the world around you.

Sometimes we mistake boredom for the discomfort that some people feel from being by themselves. If you can improve your relationship with yourself, you'll not only experience boredom much less, but you'll also look forward to having regularly scheduled alone time.

Find new things to be excited about, whether that's reading a book, cooking a meal, or doing something creative. Every moment is a blessing you spend once and never have again, make the most of them.

Being open to trying new things, though sometimes daunting, is the best way to broaden the world around you.

62 ONE PROMISE OF LIFE IS THAT IT'S GOING TO END

Our relationship with the realities in our life can be quite a roller coaster ride. It's difficult for some to cope with not getting what they want. It's very hard to admit we're full of entitlements because it makes us realize how much we take for granted. When we realize how much we take for granted, we lose the luxury of feeling sorry for ourselves. People love feeling sorry for themselves, especially when they're not getting what they want.

A lot of folks look for balance in life, as if balance itself is a checkbox on the bucket list. Instead of achieving balance, I like to look at it as continual balancing, and we'll be wobbling and stumbling our entire lives.

If you're younger and reading this, I'll let you in on a secret, it doesn't get easier as you get older, you don't feel wiser, smarter, and more in control; you just get older. As long as we're alive, we're in a constant state of imbalance, and we have to actively work try to centre things out.

It's hard to form a relationship with certain realities, they don't line up with our fantasies, or the movies, or the fairytales our parents told us when we were kids. And though it's hard, we'll still be better off fostering those relationships. We may even learn to enjoy the wobbling and stumbling, and be grateful for the opportunities to make mistakes and grow from them.

Death is one of the few things we all have in common, and that may make it our strongest bond. Living life and knowing the sand may be running out at any moment can lead to some spectacular movements.

Living life and knowing the sand may be running out at any moment can lead to some spectacular movements.

63 LOVE IS A GIFT NOT A LOAN

Don't give it out expecting it to be returned. When reciprocity is expected, can we even call that love?

I know folks that complain about the lack of support they receive. They're upset that they promote and support their peers, but don't receive the same in return. It makes the support sound like a currency.

Personally, I don't want folks supporting me who are looking for something in return. If you enjoy my stuff please share, if not, no stress.

Love and support people you want to love and support. There are people in our lives whose triumphs bring us joy; support them. If you don't particularly enjoy an individual then ignore their existence, do your thing, and keep it moving.

When folks don't live up to our expectations, bitterness and negativity can develop. Only we carry that burden, not them.

Let that sh*t go.

Focus on those you love and those that love you, disregard the rest. We're not all going to get along, that's OK.

Having people to love is a gift, don't take them for granted, and include yourself on that list. The act of loving is a gift in itself, don't take that for granted, not everyone is afforded that opportunity.

Having people to love is a gift,
don't take them for granted,
and include yourself on that list.

64 SELF-PITY IS SELF SABOTAGE

The things you are capable of are amazing, but no one can get you to realize that potential but YOU. The growth you require, in order to reach that potential, means you have to be uncomfortable.

This discomfort comes in the form of the challenges in life. When you encounter the challenge, you can either curl up into a ball, and feel miserably sorry for yourself OR you can stare at that challenge in the eye, and run towards it with everything you have.

You already know this. In your life you've encountered and overcome challenges, and the result was growth. The same circumstances aren't going to present themselves. In this video game of life, the challenges will get tougher, and one of the biggest obstacles you have to overcome is yourself.

No Pain, No Gain is cliché for a reason, and it's been used so often it has lost meaning, but the truth it holds will remain relevant forever.

If you think these words don't apply to you, and what you're going through is worse than everyone else, realize you're a spoiled brat with electricity and running water who needs to spend a week in any slum in South Africa to realize what a PROBLEM really is.

Instead of worrying about what the world is or isn't doing for you, worry about what you can do for the world, contribute in any way you can to make this rock feel like a better place for others.

In this video game of life, the challenges will get tougher, and one of the biggest obstacles you have to overcome is yourself.

65 WORMS OF VALIDATION

Have you ever talked to someone and all they do is talk about themselves?

Have you ever pay attention to the things you say? Is that all you're doing as well?

Sometimes when you step back and observe conversations, it's simply people waiting for their turn to speak, so they can relate that topic back to them. It doesn't make for a very interesting conversation, and we're all guilty of it sometimes.

This goes back to identity and how we choose to identify ourselves. Sometimes we have this need to make proclamations to describe who we are just incase people don't know. The reality is the only true indicator of who we are as people come from our actions.

It feels as if we're baby birds with our mouths open hoping for worms of validation, but our stomachs never fill. That's the danger with validation, it's an addiction with no end in sight.

We're all self-absorbed to varying degrees, and our self-interests dictate the decisions we make, but being mindful of these facts can do well to enhance our ability to interact with others.

It's OK if we don't get along with everyone; folks are like chemicals, and when they mix, the reaction can be anything. We tend not to like in others, what we don't like in ourselves, so if you come across a person you can't stand, it's beneficial to pay attention to why, for your own sake.

Talk to people you're interested in talking to, and ask them questions because learning new sh*t is fun. If they're not interesting to you, create a diversion and run away; life's too short to be around folks you don't want to be around.

Pay attention to the words and ideas you put out in the universe as well. If you are only about yourself, you'll only be left with yourself.

Pay attention to the words
and ideas you put out in the
universe as well. If you're
all about yourself, you'll
only be left with yourself.

66 WHICH WAY IS YOUR SPIRAL HEADED?

We get on a roll and then all of a sudden we get derailed. Some of us fall into slumps and it just seems that we fall deeper and deeper into an endless pit. The term rock bottom loses meaning because we never feel like we land, and once we think we've felt the worst of it, somehow it finds a way to get worse.

It's the roller coaster ride of life. There are highs and lows, but the highs and successes are always easier to be forgotten, and the failures and low points seem to haunt us a bit longer. That's the work of our mind. Unhappiness is simply when the picture in your head doesn't match the picture in front of you, and once that mismatch is discovered the gap seems to widen even more.

What can we do?

Well for starters we can adjust the picture in our head. Often times that picture includes things that are completely out of our control, like people. Maybe someone didn't treat us the way we wanted to be treated or maybe a situation didn't work out the way we hoped. These expectations and hopes are the real culprit, not the people and outcomes.

We can also adjust the picture in front of us. Every moment is a moment to try to make the life we want and change the things we dislike. Obviously this is easier said than done (I feel like I have to say that often), but what is easy these days? If you expected an easy life, you better find the person who promised you that, and punch them in the nose because they lied. Trust your struggle. Life is the struggle; the journey is the experience; the outcomes, especially when successful, will be forgotten quickly, and replaced with new things to worry about.

The fact that we have time to overthink and overanalyze things is a sure indication that we're spoiled with the leisure time to direct our resources towards creating problems instead of other things -- like surviving. The fridge has food in it, the water is coming out the pipe, no imminent external threats, so let's get existential and find some other reason to suffer.

Even the problems that may be real become inflated with our drama-queen-esque way of viewing them. Our centre of the universe complexes ensures that there cannot be problems greater than ours.

There's no magic pill or mantra that clears us of our suffering ways. Pain is a part of us just as much as our fingers and toes. How much we choose to suffer is a different story.

We decide how much of life is a tragedy or comedy, which will determine if we spiral up or down. Besides, in 100 years none of this will matter. Enjoy it while you can.

Every moment is a moment to try to make the life we want and change the things we dislike

67 HOW DO OTHERS SEE YOU?

Do you think if you walked into a room with 10 people in it they'll all see the same thing? If you told them a story, would they interpret and understand that story all the same way?

Though we don't know for sure, I think most will agree the answer is NO. Everyone is made up of their genetics and experiences, and how they react to their surroundings is as unique as their fingerprints.

Not everyone enjoys my company. Not everyone has the attention span or interest to make it to this third paragraph. Not everyone who reads this whole chapter will agree with it, let alone enjoy it. None of that is my concern. I made peace with the idea that I can't win'em all, so I just focus on doing what I enjoy, and hope like-spirited folks discover and vibe with it.

Life is too short to try to make believers out of doubters. I'd rather work towards proving my supporters right. Allowing them to see me the way they see me, and just be happy they're taking the time to check out the work and pay attention.

If people don't feel your vibe, that's OK. People-pleasing is a tiresome and pointless task. That time can be spent on more productive activities.

It feels good to be validated, accepted, and even celebrated, but success is a lousy teacher. I don't dismiss folks who aren't feeling me because some of them may have valuable jewels to help me improve. Discovering those jewels requires me to both take the time to listen to what they have to say, and evaluate that feedback with the priorities I have in my journey. If it'll help me on my way, expect a long distance thank you hug.

It's 4:30am as I type this, so I don't remember the quote, but it was something along the lines of no matter how juicy the peach is there will always be the person who just doesn't like peaches. Not everyone likes Hip Hop, not everyone likes reading long books, and not everyone likes beards (shocking eh). That's a reality I hold near and have found peace in.

I hope in your journey, you know what's important to you and realize the approval of others is never more important than your approval of yourself.

...the approval of others is never more important than your approval of yourself.

68 YOU DECIDE YOUR WORTH

I know there are a million different factors, people, situations, and outcomes that affect the way you feel about yourself, but none of them determine your worth; you do.

For those of us who've been in the heartbreak aisle of life, having someone we adore no longer share those sentiments can do much to make us feel in the gutter. The issue isn't their actions; it's our relationship with those actions. Our self worth was never bound to their approval, or affection, or attention, but it sure feels that way. We can allow these circumstances to determine our worth, but remember, it's only if we allow it.

Every moment of every day we get to determine how we feel about ourselves. Within all of us there are things worth celebrating, and things that we're not the most proud of, the choice is what we decide to focus on.

Our jobs, our income, marital status, social circle, our position in society, all of these can definitely determine how we feel about about ourselves, but none of them are true measurements of who we are. We have an identity, and how we choose to identify ourselves is up to us. Your identity is like a flag, and you can place it into anything you want.

Some place that flag in their religious beliefs or nationality; others stick it in their family tree. We are free to stick it in anything and everything we want. The important point is we get to determine where we stick it. Identity and worth are concepts created by us, and we should keep this in mind to ensure our well being.

Not everything is in our control, so it's unfair to us to allow those things to affect our self-worth.

No one determines your value but you. If you think you're a miracle or you're worthless, you're right. You decide your value.

Within all of us there are things worth celebrating, and things that we're not the most proud of, the choice is what we decide to focus on.

60 THE STORM IS IN YOUR MIND, NOT IN YOUR LIFE

We have the ever so humbling ability to see life one brief moment at a time. Sure we can see patterns and try our best to determine what may happen next, but that's no guarantee that we're right.

It only takes a moment to end our ability to have any more moments (nine months to make it, a split second to take it). Sometimes we have so many options in the present we don't know which way to go. We're scared to make the wrong decision so instead, we stay put. Where we are may not be the best place for us, but it sure is familiar, and familiar is comfortable, and who doesn't enjoy comfort.

It's an amazing world out there, but a much larger, more intricate universe inside each and every one of us. The thoughts that came from inside are what populate every syllable in every word, on every page, in every book in the world. Every building you see, and structure designed, all came from a spark of thought once upon a time. It's brilliant and terrifying at the exact same time.

We have the ability to build and destroy in our minds. We can take the smallest worry, and amplify it into a colossal set of potential problems, which in turns paralyzes us with fear. On the other hand, we can tell ourselves that even though we're in pain, we need to push harder to achieve what we've set out to accomplish. Mental strength is what makes people extraordinary.

It's inside, not outside, where we determine if we're happy, sad, lonely, overwhelmed, successful, ashamed, proud, etc. Our life circumstances are simply the things our mind reacts to in order to make these decisions. Life will never be what happens to you, but rather how you deal with the things that are happening.

The mind is a powerful thing and it's not a walk in the park to work with it. Like every muscle, or skill, it requires training and practice; real and solid results will only appear over time (no easy-quick-fixes, sorry).

Our brains don't sleep; they work even while our bodies are at rest. We can spend our lives building connections inside that will help us further navigate life on the outside. That can be done through reading, writing, dancing, traveling, meditating or any other activity that stimulates the mind.

Taking a trip into the mind of others is also an amazing exploratory adventure. I'd recommend finding people that you understand the least (these are the types we tend to avoid the most) and picking their brains to expand yours.

Our minds are our only refuge from the rest of the world. Don't be afraid to spend some quality time with yourself, you may grow to enjoy your own company.

It's inside, not outside, where
we determine if we're happy

70 PUT THAT HEART ON A LEASH

Just because your heart wants something, doesn't mean it's wise to pursue it. When it comes to our emotions, rational thinking and logic are rarely in the room when our heart is speaking to us. The language of our wants rarely focuses on what makes sense, but rather what will scratch an itch we have inside.

As someone who's pursuing his life aspirations, I'm completely down for folks to chase what their heart desires to the ends of the earth. Death is the only true deterrent, and once that occurs, it doesn't matter because the game is over.

There are a few things that we should keep in mind though.

Following our heart is simply giving into an urge that we believe needs to be quenched. It doesn't fit within the confines of making sense but more so of feeling good. Some who consider themselves to be realists have issues with this because they feel it's too idealistic and can lead to much pain. Personally, I agree to some extent, but think we need to differentiate the ideas of immediate gratification and authentic passion.

Fear is a large roadblock for our heart, and can be used as support for our brains to tell us to stay safe and avoid risk. What are we really staying safe from? Death? That can only be delayed, not avoided. Failure? That's an essential part of growth. Suffering? That's an essential tool for survival. Playing it safe doesn't ensure anything in a universe where we have very little control.

Your heart is not your heart; it's just a romanticized label for another part of your brain. It's not a simple black and white idea that we're using logic versus love. There are multiple parts of our psyche that come into play everyday when we interact with ourselves and the outside world.

We're highly self-indulged animals, and are pretentious enough to believe that everything and everyone was created for our bidding. This is one of the reasons we internalize and relive our suffering so much. It's a *Why Me?* complex, that allows us to ignore those around us, and focus solely on the pointless things that are bothersome in our lives.

There isn't a RIGHT way to live your life. Even if you make an unwise decision, you have the power to turn that into gold. Only you know the desires that exist inside you, and if those desires don't result in harm and exploitation of others, then they may be worth exploring. People want to make up stereotypical death bed regrets, but really the only one I can think of is that we may not enjoy the end of a life we didn't bother taking the time to design the way we wanted.

Is this an easy task? No. Is it worth it? For Sure (if I read your mind, you owe me another $5).

Don't be afraid to get hurt, it's part of life; it's only unnecessary if there's nothing to learn from it, and there's always something to learn from it if your mind is open enough.

Don't be afraid to get hurt,
it's part of life; it's only
unnecessary if there's
nothing to learn from it.

71

ARE YOU IN IT TO GIVE OR RECEIVE?

They (I dunno who they are) say relationships need to be give and take. The relationships we kick ourselves over are the ones we felt we gave so much, and received so little.

When people evaluate their relationships, they talk about what they're looking for, almost as if they're posting up a job ad or something. They list requirements and priorities hoping to find a match. The mindset is focused on what they want more so than what they have to give.

This mindset can lead to our givings being conditional upon the receiving. That leads to those unhealthy relationships where everyone feels under appreciated.

The culture of consumerism and entitlement that we've been exposed to, has definitely encouraged a *Get Yours* mentality that is weakening the foundation of the relationships we have with each other. It appears more difficult for people now to function as a unit because once a member's needs aren't being met, they skate away. This culture can encourage people to replace instead of repair.

Instead of listing the things you're looking for, list the things you want to give, and not on the condition of getting anything in return. Give for the sake of giving, there's no competition or obstacle when you want to share, only when you want to take for yourself.

There are individuals that were once in my life that are no longer around, but I know they're in better situations now. Those better situations don't have beards like me, but those situations fit the priorities they have much better than a guy like me ever could. I genuinely care about them, and I'm happy that they've been able to move to a situation that's better suited for them.

There's an abundance of people in my life I can give to and care little about receiving anything in return from; we all have them. I, not only get to determine who these people are, I get to determine what I'm willing to share and invest into them. It's OK to say no, and contrary to what people tell you, it's completely fine, if not recommended, to put yourself first. Love doesn't hurt people, people hurt people.

Ask yourself why you're entering into the relationships you're in. If you've placed expectations on the other person, you've also set a situation where disappointments can run rampant. People are human; they will make mistakes and have changes of heart, that's a promise. It's not fair to put that pressure on them, and you definitely do not want that pressure on yourself.

If you want to put your energy and efforts into something and expect something in return, focus on projects and problems that need solving. Those outcomes will depend solely on the energy you give them.

All the things you're looking to receive from someone else you can give to yourself, especially love; you'll have so much, you'll have no choice but to find people to share it with.

All the things you're looking to receive from someone else you can give to yourself, especially love.

72

FIGHT!

This is your life, fight for it.

Whatever you're feeling and going through, if it's not the feelings and position you want to be in, you have to be prepared to fight your way out. Every inch has to be earned. It doesn't matter if the dude next door is so much better off, and everyone seems luckier than you. Those are irrelevant to the life you want. For the life you want, you have to focus and be prepared to fight.

You're going to realize very quickly the biggest battles you fight are with yourself. I'm talking about all the negative thoughts, the excuses, the procrastination, the fears, and the doubts. These things are in you. I don't know why they're there, but they are. You can't rid yourself of them, but you can move forward in life by overcoming them one fight at a time.

Recognizing your enemy is one thing. Being prepared to punch it square in the nose without hesitation is an other. This is your life, no one else's. Your value, your direction, and your purpose are all determined by YOU. Greatness is developed and earned, and tough decisions and sacrifices will have to be made. The obligations you feel you have to others do not allow you to pawn off responsibility for your life on to them. As selfish as it may sound, you need to do what's best for yourself first. Only when you're able to take care of yourself can you help those around you effectively. Fight for yourself and those around you.

None of us are victims. Every breath our lungs allow is an opportunity to turn things around and gain momentum. It's a fight, it's not going to be easy, and it most definitely will not be fair. Do what needs to be done, claw for every inch of the life you want. The spirals in life can go both up and down. Recognize the toxic people, places, and choices in your life, and muster up the courage to get rid of them. That may not be what you want to hear, but that's what needs to happen.

We're all getting knocked down in this fight of life, but not all of us are working to get back up. Some simply stay down and wait until the clock runs out. Do you want to be one of them?

You're going to realize very quickly the biggest battles you fight are with yourself.

73 YOU NEED TO FORGIVE

It's an absolute essential practice to ensure you're not holding any grudges. Those grudges pull you down.

Forgiving others (and I mean TRULY forgiving them) is not condoning what someone did to you, it's making the decision that you will no longer allow that bullsh*t to hold you down.

We've all had horrible things done to us, and honestly, we may have also done horrible things to others. Think about how toxic it is to continue reliving those moments, filling your present tense with regret, pain, and eventual depression.

Mental anguish has physical consequences, and these can take days off your life. Holding this stuff on your shoulders is a burden only you hold, not the person you're holding the grudge against.

Nelson Mandela said that it's like drinking poison and hoping it kills the other person.

We all f*ck up. Rather than continually beating yourself up over it, forgive yourself. Letting go of the past will give you more of everything to create your future.

This is in no way, shape, or form that is easy, but it's worth it. I still hold pain for transgressions of the past, and it's a daily reminder to let it go. I'm only hurting myself by reliving them. Forgiving is a personal exercise, and doesn't need to be announced or shared. You need to truly forgive to feel it. We've all done it. There's things we cared about five years ago, but can laugh it off now. Make the choices that allow you to laugh this stuff off even earlier.

I love you for taking the time to read this, and it feels awesome to know that you enjoy the writing, which further motivates me to share the stuff that helped me. There will always be people in the world that will exploit your need to care and share. Don't let them kill that in you. Take risks, keep meeting new people, and you'll meet people that deserve and appreciate the love you want to shower; it won't be all of them, but that's life.

Forgive yourself and forgive others. You deserve a life free from such pointless burdens.

Forgive yourself and forgive others. You deserve a life free from such pointless burdens.

74 LABELS ARE DEHUMANIZING

Faggot, slut, nigger, terrorist, bitch, hobo, them, us, Sikh, Hindu, Punjabi, atheist, Christian, American, Patriot, Sunni, Shia, infidel, Singh, Khalsa, Jatt, etc., we all use them, and though they're generally used to label fellow human beings, they do a wonderful job of making them seem a little less like us.

Those minor changes in perception towards others go a long way. Couple that with our general inclination towards being around people that look, think, talk, walk, act, and agree like us, and we create a collection of imaginary lines, making for some very real segregation.

A lot of people think this is just an accident that can be remedied with some educational videos and a couple of peace signs, but that's the farthest from the truth. Divide and conquer has been a tactic used for centuries to keep things in order. The news does an amazing job of teaching us who to fear and who to hate, and we do a horrible job of asking ourselves, "Should I be buying all this?"

II saw this amazing speaker, and he said something fascinating, "KNOWING is out of style, and BELIEVING is in fashion; we need to bring KNOWING back in style." We need not confuse what we know versus what has been poured into our brains over and over by our parents, society, media, and other influences. I only came to this realization after working with kids, and watching them regurgitate their parents' teachings as if they were programmed out of a box.

Every label we hold, every label we stick on others, every label we judge is not real. They're not real, but they're effective. These labels do a wonderful job of making the 'others' less like us and easier to care less for.

We tend to care about those we see ourselves in the most. Though masked as compassion, it's really a morbid self-interest. It's psychology though, and it applies to all of us; so it's nothing to thumb our noses down on, but it is something we're better off recognizing.

I'm not an idealist. The practice of labeling won't be going away anytime soon. However, if we know we can shed one or two and open ourselves up to those we viewed as different, I promise, with every molecule of my being, our human experience will be that much richer.

"KNOWING is out of style, and BELIEVING is in fashion; we need to bring KNOWING back in style."

75 CELEBRATE YOUR SCARS

You are not a victim. You are a survivor in this adventure called life. So things didn't go your way, you were injured, you were used, exploited, tossed aside, but you're reading this, so you survived. You're a f*cking champ.

Life doesn't begin after the obstacles, life IS the obstacles. We have our escapes, but reality is much more beautiful. Things aren't going to always go our way. If we feel entitled to things, we're going to have a bad time.

Nothing is promised. When that idea is honestly absorbed, every moment is celebrated and appreciated.

Appreciation is so essential, and if you're too busy feeling sorry for yourself to find things to appreciate, then your misery is not only guaranteed, it's deserved.

Our pursuits of happiness aren't certain. We're simply chasing things and people we feel will accomplish that goal. They rarely do, but we'll keep chasing just in case.

It's a wild ride, a bumpy ride, and you're not going to come from it unscathed. Why would you want to? Solid learning comes the hard way. Those bumps, bruises, scars, and wounds were earned, and valuable lessons are attached to them.

This life you have isn't a problem to be solved, it's an experience to be soaked in. There's no purpose in this life beyond the one you choose to give it, and even that purpose is permitted to change whenever your heart desires it.

Change is scary, so what? Do you want to avoid scary things so you can arrive at death safely? Don't take yourself too seriously. You're a bag of blood, bones, and meat floating on a spinning rock; enjoy the ride. People that tell you any different are simply reinforcing their choices. I'm telling you this to reinforce mine.

Enjoy your present; you don't get the moments back. You are who you are and can create your own smiles. Don't put the key to your happiness in someone else's pocket.

You're getting wiser everyday, celebrate that!

I'm not telling you anything you don't already know; I just want you to know you deserve to remember it.

Change is scary, so what?
Do you want to avoid
scary things so you can
arrive at death safely?

76 VALIDATION IS A HELLUVA DRUG

It's a consistency among us to have some concern about how we're perceived by other people. It's a bit too cliché and absolute to be like, "I don't give a f*ck what anyone thinks of me," because really everyone cares. However, I do think it's a bit too intense to concern yourself with the thoughts of others, as they're not really thinking about you as much as you think.

That mustard stain on your new shirt will not (and should not) be the make or break of your day. Sh*t happens, people drop food on their clothes. I'd be lying if I didn't acknowledge the superficial world that exists, but the people we worry about are also worried about what we think of them. Many of the people we encounter enjoy our company for the simple way we make them feel. In those instances, concerning ourselves with appeasing them is unnecessary.

Be yourself. Not everyone is going to dig your style, your demeanor, or your overall energy; and that's OK. You'll be better off with the few people that like you for who you are, compared to having a grand sum of people who will only like you if you become something else. Even among the people reading this, there are people that want me to be more than I am. I may lose them if I don't make those changes, but I'm fine with that.

I don't get along with everyone, and everyone doesn't get a long with me. Life is too short to worry about that. Take the time to be around the people that enjoy your company, life is more enjoyable that way.

I watched an interview today with a musician who said, "10% of

222

every group of people you'll enjoy," doesn't matter if they're a hipster or high society, if you put yourself out there you'll find a tenth that you enjoy, so try it out.

I create, write, and present things to the public. It'd be preposterous for me to get all, "Imma do me, y'all like it or not, I don't care." I like listening to the folks that take the time to soak my stuff in. The feedback that agrees with, and enhances me gets worked in; the rest floats away with the wind.

Don't worry about what others think because there's too many of them to cater to. Worry about being comfortable in your own skin and those who appreciate that will connect with you.

Worry about being comfortable
in your own skin and those
who appreciate that will
connect with you.

FAKE IT 'TIL YOU MAKE IT

There's an assumption that the most successful people are void of the feelings the rest of us have; the fear, the anxiety, the doubt, the depression, and the lack of motivation. This is not true. Success isn't simply a circumstance, how can you even begin to quantify it? For some, waking up in the morning is success, and for others, it won't exist unless it's followed with seven zeroes. Feel free to quantify your success, if anything, you're better off and more focused for it.

Some use vision boards, which are completed with detailed information as to what they want to achieve. My good friend, and the ever so inspirational Lilly Singh (a.k.a. iiSuperWomanii), showed me her vision board, and realized that she had accomplished many of the things written on there. Was that an indication that she was successful? No. It was an indication that she needed to update the board with her new goals, milestones, and metrics. Healthy ambition is climbing a peakless mountain, while enjoying the view every step of the way.

The negative feelings we all have can be addictive, just as the positive. It's up to us to decide which ones we want to choose and feed. Physical activity is essential (as I type this, my gym membership is expired so when you run into me, ask me if I've renewed it, and punch me in the shoulder if I say, "No"). Your current circumstances may not align with your definition of success, but that's temporary if you actually get up, start, and get things moving.

If life was awesome and you felt like a million bucks, what would you be doing with your time? If you can't do that activity for eight hours yet, do it for two. Progress will add up if you stick with it. As with anything, progress and improvements take time. We can't have high expectations and low patience. Baby steps in the right direction will get you where you want to be.

They say dress for the job you want, fake it till you make it. It's not simply faking it, it's making the mental adjustments now to help you bring yourself to the place you want to be.

The negative feelings we all have can be addictive, just as the positive. It's up to us to decide which ones we want to choose and feed.

78 BABY STEPS ADD UP

I meet so many people with high expectations and low patience. This is the recipe for failure.

Whether it is business, music, fitness, or even building a relationship, it starts with a first step, and only grows with the steps after that; there is no autopilot.

I've reached the level I'm at with those baby steps. I'm nowhere close to my aspirations. I plan to perform in stadiums within the decade, but that's only going to happen with the small steps I'm taking this year, this month, this week, this day, and this moment.

Maturity and patience comes with time, and with that time also comes the realization that there isn't much time to make things happen. We tend to put things off because we're scared. Scared of what? Well whatever our imagination can create to keep us from taking that next baby step.

The fears that prevent us from taking those steps are only conquered by taking those steps. Buildings are built brick by brick, poems are written word by word, and relationships grow day by day. Respect the time necessary for things to take place, and realize if you lack that respect, you really don't deserve sh*t.

It's the journey that's important, not the destination. The destination for all of us is death. Our credits will be rolling soon, and all that will have mattered is what happened every step before the end, if anything at all.

It's never too late to start building the life you want. The recipe for success is simple: act, learn, build, and repeat. Realize you've been using this recipe your entire life for your accomplishments, whether it was learning how to walk or learning how to read; it all took time. Our achievements feel easy after the fact and impossible before. Recognize this concept and move forward despite it.

Also, find people in the same mindset of taking baby steps. It's much better than keeping the company of folks who still have grand expectations and excuses to match. They'll only waste your time.

It's never too late to start building the life you want.

70
YOU ONLY HAVE SO MUCH TIME

You can only make so many people happy, and no matter what you do, some folks will never be satisfied because they depend on you for their happiness, which is selfish of them. They're toxic, and you'll be better off without them. Put yourself first, it's not selfish.

Expecting others to put you first; that is selfish.
You're writing your story right now.

If your life were a movie, would anyone want to watch it? Our favorite movies always have our hero overcoming challenges and becoming better for it. Are you trying to overcome your challenges or running from anything that is remotely uncomfortable?

In this day and age where everyone is praised and congratulated for every little accomplishment, I think it would be important to focus on those who are still trying to overcome the obstacles. Instead of celebrating the winners, let's celebrate those who are trying to win, still uncomfortable, grinding, earning every inch they receive. Encouragement goes a long way.

Everything I do comes from the support you show me. The legacy of Humble The Poet won't be based on Kanwer Singh's work; it'll be more a result of the relationships and connections that were formed between myself and all of you throughout this journey. I appreciate you all immensely and that connection keeps me working harder and harder to reach the next milestone.

Things tend to look easy after they're done and impossible before. Every person with aspirations will hit obstacles and meet naysayers. It's up to us to decide whether we want to focus on those telling us why we should give up, or those that are pushing us along the way with their positivity. It's also up to us to decide if we're helping others on the way, or giving them reasons to throw in the towel.

I don't know what my story will be like when it's all said and done. When I'm dead, my legacy won't be of much importance to me. Although I do know that I would not be able to exist in the present peacefully, knowing that I gave up on exploring what I have inside simply because things became difficult.

I'm a survivor, so are you, it's what's makes us a special form of life on this planet, we adapt, change and grow to enhance our ability to exist and thrive.

We all have the ability to be the heroes of our own story.

It's up to us to decide
on whether we want to
focus on those telling us
why we should give up.

80 DON'T INFECT YOURSELF WITH NEGATIVITY

Negativity is a disease – don't infect yourself

I'm dead serious, life is challenging enough maneuvering around the negativity of others; it's almost hopeless if that negativity is coming from within.

Doubts, fears, and any thoughts that aren't pushing you forward will do well to hold you back. They're just thoughts, but those thoughts will have an impact on you. Negative thoughts are bad for your health, and will hinder your growth.

Be mindful of negative people; if you love yourself, cut them loose before they begin to rub off on you (and they will). Some of you will disagree, and remark that it's the responsibility of positive folks to help the negative folks, to those I bid the best of luck to you. My changes didn't happen from others forcing their energy upon me, it came from time and realizing things from within. Our time is limited so be mindful of who you spend it on. If you're being positive, and those around you enjoy being negative, find new people to be around.

Attitude plays a huge part in our lives, and the way we feel about it. From the moment we wake up, we decide whether we have something to hop out of our bed towards, or whether we need to hit the snooze button, hoping those extra nine minutes of sleep feels like two hours.

Negative thoughts are toxic, take the time to identify them, and show them the door. We all have them, and we'll never be immune to them, but we can be mindful and make wise decisions when we encounter them.

There are other wonderful germs to spread -- love, ambition, inspiration, and positivity. Find those within you, and infect those around you.

Our time is limited, so be
mindful of who you spend it on.

81 WORDS ARE WEAPONS, IF YOU ALLOW THEM TO BE

I'm not going to talk about how to handle the words of others when they attack our feeble egos. It's a given, our egos are hungry, we're whores for validation, and that opens us up to be vulnerable to less ideal situations, especially when someone says something we don't want to hear.

Instead, let's talk about the words we put out in the universe. We all understand the power of words, and how they can affect those around us, but how many of us are using that power with intent? It costs nothing to dish out some extra compliments here and there. They don't have to be forced or disingenuous, look for something that inspires a positive reaction. If I see someone made an effort to dress up, I compliment their outfit, or earrings, or shoes.

We have the power to add a smile to someone's face, just as much as we can inspire a frown, laughter, frustration, peace, or clarity. People won't remember what you said; they'll remember how you made them feel. Instead of worrying about what people think about you, make an active effort to make them feel from you.

Not everyone gets along as well as others. Find those you gel with and spread some sunshine their way. Let it come through not only in your words, but your actions. Nothing is an obligation, only help those you want, and help them in the way you want.

Small words and gestures go a long way...

People won't remember what you said, they'll remember how you made them feel.

82 YOU ARE A WORK OF ART IN PROGRESS

Every moment is a brushstroke on that masterpiece of your life. It won't be completed, until your life is completed. Fortunately and unfortunately you won't be here to see the final product.

That final product was never for you. You are simply a part of this creation adding to the creation. We don't live in this universe; we are the universe.

"If you want to find the secrets of the universe, think in terms of energy, frequency and vibration." — Nikola Tesla

There's nothing to solve, ponder and search for. Energy, frequencies and vibrations are felt; these cannot be created or destroyed, they can only be changed. This is one of those brief moments when science and spirituality can hold hands. Listen to your feelings, trust your struggles, it's how everything in this universe tends to work.

Our realities exist within us. Our beliefs are simply beliefs, and everyday impossible seems to be a temporary word. You're going to meet a myriad of folks who want to tell you your purpose. They may have the best of intentions, or simply want someone to affirm the path they've taken, or maybe they just want company. The purpose you give your life is the purpose your life holds.

I'm not here to preach a philosophy or teach lessons. I'm here to take the pills that are tough to swallow and find a way to make them easier to digest. Life prescribes those pills, and they'll be shoved down your throat whether you like it or not. . The moments I experience will be different from yours, I have no place, or faith in myself to even begin to understand you beyond what we have in common, which is simply what's in our nature.

One alarming thing we seem to have in common (in the first world at least) is an unlimited ability to be ungrateful, which results in a lack of smiles. We can't smile all the time, but many people wouldn't mind adding a few more everyday here and there. It's not a secret to do so... appreciate, appreciate, appreciate.

Nothing in this universe is our friend, and nothing in this universe is our enemy because nothing in this universe is separate from us. We are the drop in the ocean, and the ocean in the drop (word to Rumi).

Find reasons to be happy or find reasons to be miserable, I'm confident you can do both well. If you're looking for the easy road get acquainted with the word monotony.

Paint your picture the way you want it painted, it's your canvas, don't let anyone else hold the brush.

Paint your picture the way you want it painted, it's your canvas, don't let anyone else hold the brush.

83 LOSING A PIECE OF OURSELVES

When we lose someone special in our lives, it feels like they take a piece of us with them. We can feel like a shell of our former selves, mainly because the life we spent time building with that person no longer exists.

Some consider this is a feeling of emptiness; I consider it a cleaning of our canvas. Emotionally it may feel like we're losing, but really we're just being jolted out of a familiar zone we have.

Though it feels like we miss the person, often what we really miss is how that person made us feel about ourselves. If relationships make us feel like we were worthy, we may lose that feeling of worth once those relationships end. I know the feeling sucks, but it isn't wise to avoid those unpleasant emotions, as they generally are what usher us into growth.

I'm not here to write words to make it feel better, I wouldn't dare deny you the growing pains. Rather, I just want you to realize that once the emotions have exhausted themselves, and there's some room for logic, these are some of the thoughts to ponder.

The most important relationship we need to foster is the one with ourselves, and every time someone else has the power to disrupt that, we should pay attention to why. No one else gets to determine your value, your worth, your mood, or your happiness, but YOU. Be mindful of who you allow in.

The stronger our relationship with ourselves, the less dependent we become on others, and the healthier those relationships actually become.

I know the feeling sucks, but it isn't wise to avoid those unpleasant emotions, as they generally are what usher us into growth.

84 DON'T BE TOO HARD ON YOURSELF

I'm never bothered by negative comments of others because things I say to myself are much harsher. It's a difficult juggling act trying to stay disciplined without proverbially smacking yourself up every so often.

As a teacher, with the kids, I would celebrate their efforts more than their achievements. Maybe that would be a great thing to do for ourselves. After all, we know if we're giving it all we can give.

There's satisfaction from knowing you worked your ass off, you gave it all you got, and left it all in the ring, regardless of the outcome. Life's a lot like poker; making wise decisions will definitely help you out, but sometimes, even if you do everything right, things may still not turn out in your favor (it's always that river card gotdammit). That's just a reality of life, nothing is promised, and good intentions neither guarantee nor warrant positive outcomes.

Many of the injuries we suffer mentally can be self--inflicted. Having negative thoughts about yourself can become a self-fulfilling prophecy. It's difficult to have constant positive thoughts, it can even appear a bit cocky to the outside world, but the self-love and self support is worth it. Cockiness and confidence will always have a fine line, so we're better off accepting that some may never realize there's a difference between the two.

It's in our best interest to be the head cheerleader on our spirit team. The smoke and mirrors people put up to project a level of success is something we know we can't do, we'll be only fooling ourselves. The more conversations we have within, the better equipped we are of recognizing our true being.

It's a tough enough job keeping ourselves happy, let alone others. We generally tend to be our toughest critics, but that tough love leads to beautiful outcomes, just don't overdo it.

Having negative thoughts about yourself can become a self-fulfilling prophecy.

85 WHAT'S RIGHT AND WRONG?

I'm not even concerned with what your morals are. I think it's more interesting to find out WHERE those morals came from.

We all hold different positions on what we feel is right and wrong. Some of us can even admit how flexible those positions are.

Never make the mistake of assuming illegal means immoral. It used to be illegal for women to vote, black folks to sit at the front of the bus. In some parts of the world, it's still illegal for girls to go to school.

Think for yourself, pay attention to where your values come from, and respect that not everyone sees it your way. Don't judge people just because they don't share your worldview.

Thinking in absolutes is simplistic and an insult to complex grey matter that exists between your ears. The world isn't black and white, it's many shades of grey,

Think for yourself, pay
attention to where your values
come from, and respect that
not everyone sees it your way

86 EMBRACE YOUR CHALLENGES

When you were a baby learning to walk, you fell repeatedly. Learning to read didn't happen overnight; neither did any other skill you have today that feels like second nature. The challenges we face are the opportunities to grow into better people.

When you get a flat tire, you don't slash the other three. When you hit a challenge in life, you don't fall down and give up; you push back. We're animals, and we have the ability to conquer many of the challenges that come our way.

Much of the game is mental. Though overcoming many challenges isn't the easiest thing, no one promised you life was going to be easy, and if you want to move forward in it, you need to have the mindset to welcome challenges and tackle them as they come.

Changes and interruptions to our normally scheduled programming are inevitable. Just because change is uncomfortable doesn't mean it isn't going to happen. The best thing is to learn to work with change instead of resisting it, since resistance is really futile.

The best version of you is peeled away and developed. You don't become your best straight out the box. The challenges in life are needed to bring out your potential.

When things get difficult, remind yourself to see the opportunities, and not just the challenges.

The best version of you is peeled away and developed. You don't become your best straight out the box. The challenges in life are needed to bring out your potential.

87 HOW RARELY THEY THINK OF US

We wouldn't care about what others think of us if we realize how rarely they did.

We use our imaginations to assume what folks MAY think of us in various situations. Those judgments are really a reflection of us much more than the person we're projecting them on.

Basing even a pinch of your happiness on the approval of others forfeits it. Life isn't American Idol, you're not auditioning, and even in those rare instances where someone else's opinion can determine your future (job interviews, American Idol auditions, meeting the in-laws), you're still better off being yourself and allowing the confidence that comes with that to shine.

You'll never be able to make everyone happy, trying to do so is a key ingredient to failure. Speak your truth, and speak it loud, and surround yourself with those that encourage you to be the person you want to be.

Write your own story, pave your own highway. I'm most impressed by folks who AREN'T trying to impress me. That type of honesty is attractive and empowering, and everyone on the planet is capable of it.

Those that really matter will never give you a hoop to jump through.

You'll never be able to make everyone happy, trying to do so is a key ingredient to failure.

88 LOVE AND LOGIC WON'T HOLD HANDS

Someone shared a cool analogy with me today. They said our brains are like chocolate covered peanuts, the peanut being our brain (I think she was hinting at something), and the chocolate being our emotions.

That emotional coating causes quite a bit of duality within us. This is very obvious in matters of love, but also in the general day-to-day scheme of things.

Procrastination is an idea of what I *want* to do versus what I *need* to do. Fear holds us back from doing many of the things we fully know will move us forward. Everyone knows it's good to stay fit, but not everyone hits the gym. Emotions are a very important thing we need to explore ourselves, especially if our logic is ever to have a chance of getting a word in.

This isn't an exclusive trait to humans; animals can also defy instincts when dealing with emotional issues. My friend's dog stopped eating for days after the passing of her mother. Emotions are a powerful fuel to making things happen, but they can also stop things in their tracks.

We all let our emotions get the best of us, some say that's what makes us human. Clearly we all aren't equipped with the same emotional barometer as we all respond to things differently.

Emotions are the ups, downs, twists, and turns on the roller coaster of life. Without them, we'd be robots, and things wouldn't be as exciting. As with everything, be conscious of your emotions, as they can override your daily functions often enough to mess sh*t up.

Work with them, repressing emotions doesn't always help; it may only defer the issues for a later (and probably less convenient) time.

Sometimes the best way to deal with issues of our heart is to take the advice we would give others.

Sometimes it's just as simple as holding our breath for 10 seconds, taking a long walk, popping bubble wrap or punching a hole in the wall. Some choices will have more expensive consequences than others, and with that, a life lesson (as with every not-so-responsible choice).

Waiting 24 hours to act gives your peanut a chance to get a say, which may be your saving grace.

However you deal with the duality of your heart and mind, just remember it's an ongoing process, I feel it's getting a bit easier as I get older, or maybe that's just time gifting me a thicker skin from the bullsh*t of my past. It's all essential.

Emotions are a very important thing we need to explore ourselves, especially if our logic is ever to have a chance of getting a world in.

89 SMILE TO FEEL IT OR CONCEAL IT?

Do you ever feel like everyone else has it better than you? They don't. They're just doing the same thing you are, putting their best face forward.

We all have struggles, stresses, regrets, and anxieties. Some of us share them, some of us don't. It's real life and none of us are immune to it, but assuming no one else is going through the same things we are can amplify the problems we encounter.

What we see in other people is a highlight reel of their life. We then make ourselves more miserable by comparing that to our behind the scenes.

The key word is COMPARING.

Realize much of the frustrations we have in our present moment happen because we judge ourselves in comparison to others. Being mindful of that can save us from some of that heartache.

The key word is SOME.

I do endorse the practice of throwing on a smile. There are therapeutic benefits of just forcing your facial muscles to do it, but you'll be better off remembering reasons to smile than simply faking it.

What we see in other people is a highlight reel of their life. We then make ourselves more miserable by comparing that to our behind the scenes.

90 KILLING EXPECTATIONS BIRTHS HAPPINESS

The less expectations you have, the better off you are. It would be simple minded to speak in complete absolutes. Expectations are not always the enemy. Ambition comes from expectation, and that doesn't sit well with being content and happy.

Wanting less will make you happier than getting more, but getting more gets you more; and much of our progress as a species comes from our discontent with our current situation.

This is where you have to have that honest conversation with yourself, and ask the question, "What do I really want?"

If you want to be happy, that's a choice, and the process can begin by reducing the amount of sh*t you desire in your life. If you want to move ahead, there needs to be a level of discomfort and malcontent. The unhappiness in itself can serve as a fuel to move you ahead, and you'll see some of the most ambitious folks to ever walk the earth were never satisfied and kept moving forward.

It kind of comes off as a paradox, but it's really not. We're not wired to be happy all the time. Happiness is a mood, but most of us associate it with what's happening in our lives, rather than how we CHOOSE to react to those happenings.

I don't subscribe to the existence of ever lasting happiness. It's a wonderful and desirable idea, as well as a great marketing tool for movies, television and religions, but very illogical. There's utility in all the emotions we feel and it's up to us to actively utilize them as the gifts they can be.

Anytime you are disappointed, try to identify the expectation that wasn't met, and ask yourself if it was an expectation worth having in the first place. The disappointment itself, can serve as motivation to lace up your boots and take another stab at it. It can also serve as a lesson that maybe it's time to revisit reality, and strengthen that relationship.

It always starts with being honest with yourself...

You'll see some of the most ambitious folks to ever walk the earth were never satisfied and kept moving forward.

01 WHAT'S TAKING UP SPACE IN YOUR LIFE?

There's limited room in your life, what are you going to allow to take up space?

Happiness is simply realizing things we appreciate, but if we're too busy occupying space with things to worry about, then there won't be much room to be happy.

Don't tell me what's important, don't tell me what's realistic, all of that is arbitrary in the grand scheme of things. What's that grand scheme you ask? It's that continual promise we try to ignore, the promise that this life will come to an end.

For me, that means the few moments I have of existence should not be wasted worrying. Am I immune of worry, not at all; anyone who says they are is probably lying or selling something. What I am though, is mindful that the limited space in my life needs to be filled with things that make me smile. Since my life mainly exists in my head, the only way I can fill it up is to choose the things I focus on.

If that means cutting off toxic relationships, friends or family, then so be it. If that means being honest with myself, and no longer making excuses for the life I have, so be it. If it means shortening this journey, by taking all the risks in the world, then that's how I'll choose to live. The only person that can make you excited to get out of bed in the morning is YOU.

Create the life you want, delete the things you don't enjoy, or accept what you have. Sounds easy, but very difficult to do. On the bright side, you have your entire life to keep trying, however long or short that is.

The only person that can make
you excited to get out of bed
in the morning is YOU.

92 LIVING THE WIDTH OF YOUR LIFE

Do you want to simply live the length of your life or the width as well?

What are you capable of? I don't know, your mama don't know, neither do your encouraging teachers, or friends. But you do.

Our time is on a budget, and like all budgets, you use it or lose it. Bruce Lee died at 33, but he seems immortal because he spent that length living the width, and accomplishing in that time what many of us have only dreamed.

Great individuals have the same amount of time as we do in a day. They have the same amount of hours and minutes in a day, but for many reasons they choose to spend those hours and minutes very differently.

The person who cures cancer for good could be reading this right now, or watching TV in the other room. Even in Sikh Heritage, the third Guru didn't get into the game until his 70s. It's never too late to start, and *finishing last* is better than *didn't finish*, which is better than *didn't start*.

Jay Z said in a newer track, "Don't be good m'n*gga, be great." What greatness lies within you? Do you have it in you to share it with the world?

We're not all here for the same reasons, nor do we know the purpose of others, unless they've revealed it.

Go on... be great.

What greatness lies within you? Do you have it in you to share it with the world?

03
THE MORE LOVE YOU GIVE, THE MORE YOU GET?

I don't know you, but I do know love is a special currency. It's endless, and you can choose to spend it on whomever you please. There's no limit to how much love you can spend on a person, or the amount of people you spend loving (don't mistake love for time and energy though; that's a whole other thought).

Receiving love is important. We all want to be loved. How we go about acquiring that love (or rather people to love) is where the problem can arise.

Love is a gift, not a loan, you don't give it out, expecting it to be returned. I've learned this lesson on numerous occasions through my own follies, not to mention hearing others complain with endless stories of not getting what they put in. They feel under-appreciated, they feel their relationships are one sided and they're getting the short end of the stick. The issue here isn't the dynamic of their relationships; it's the motives behind it.

Once a gift becomes an obligation, it's no longer a gift (Merry Xmas). If you expect love, or feel obligated to love in return, then how real is it? We're all guided by self-interests, but maybe you should be interested in giving more than receiving. If the idea of sharing love without reciprocity isn't appealing to you, maybe you should re-evaluate those you share your love with, or why you want THEIR love to begin with.

I don't know too many mothers who are getting back what they're putting in with their babies. Could any of us repay that if we tried? I think at best, we could pay it forward if we decided to have children of our own, and once we do, do we even require anything in return?

Everyone has a different definition of love. Some of this love is lifelong and unconditional, other types of love die after a few arguments or if a prettier girl walks by. Personally, I don't hold much weight to the idea, as it's just an idea. Any dream-chaser will tell you that ideas are worthless; it's all in the execution.

If you have a valuable view of love, and want it in abundance, the execution shouldn't be measured in how much love you throw out there, it should be measured in how much love you let in.

The love in our lives comes from multiple sources, in varying degrees, and in so many different forms.

It may come as a kiss on the cheek, or a kick in the ass. It may be a heartfelt letter from someone who appreciates your music, to the intricate critique given by someone who doesn't want to admit they combed through your songs four times to pick out flaws.

If you have a valuable view of love, and want it in abundance, the execution shouldn't be measured in how much love you throw out there, it should be measured in how much love you let in.

94 THE ONLY CONSTANT

We treat change like it's a big deal, when it's really one of the only constants in our lives.

Some change happens quickly while others happen gradually over time, very unnoticed; nonetheless it's still change. Sometimes we prompt the change, sometimes change happens, and we have to adjust to it, these are things no one is immune to, we are experts at handling change, but we keep forgetting that.

Some of you reading this are in a situation you don't want to be in, it could be work, your health, a relationship, or life in general. You want to change, but can't seem to find the motivation to do so. There isn't much motivation needed when you want to change bad enough. Some have such an attachment to the familiar that those feelings trump their need to change, and thus, they settle.

Settling is death, please don't settle.

Doing the same things everyday will most likely have the same outcomes everyday. For outcomes to change, we need to change the things we do.

When we encourage ourselves to change for our own betterment, we're also improving our ability to adapt to the ever-changing world around us. Seasons change, friendships change, passions change, beliefs change, life changes. Many times, those changes won't catch us off guard, if we open ourselves to see them coming.

Folks will change when they're ready; there isn't much good coming from pushing them too soon. You'll end up with a headache and bruised friendship. On the same tip, I do urge anyone who is surrounded by people who continually want them to change, to change the people they surround themselves with. The approval you need is your own.

Every moment is an opportunity to shed an old self to showcase the new. We evolve as people, and those evolutions are worth celebrating. If you're feeling the need to move to a new self, but feel bound to the person you once were, realize you're not being held, but rather you're holding on.

Just let go.

Settling is death,
please don't settle.

95 NO MINIMUMS ON APPRECIATION

There's no minimum quantity when it comes to appreciation.

There's also no maximum when it comes to how much we can take for granted. Happiness is a mindset, and that mind is set by what we choose to focus on. Are we thankful for what (or who) we have, or tortured by what (or who) we don't?

When we look at it this way, happiness is no longer acquired or achieved, but instead, realized and chosen. People will often bear hug their misery, sabotaging opportunities for appreciation and happiness, for the simple fact that those feelings are familiar and comfortable.

If we feel like we're constantly collecting and acquiring to fulfill a hunger for happiness then maybe we're going about it the wrong way. The happiest people are the ones who have that magic amount of *enough* in their life (enough being their own definition).

I'm writing this from India, and I'm witnessing laughter and smiles in some of the most unsuspecting, darkest places. I also see tears and frowns in some of the most sought after, fancy locales. This isn't always the case, but it is showing how important of a role our minds play in the process.

We may be happier wanting less than getting more, but words like less, more, and happy will all have different meanings to us. The one thing I can promise though is if the word *appreciate* isn't being thrown around much, neither will those happy feelings.

t

If we feel like we're constantly
collecting and acquiring to
fulfill a hunger for happiness
then maybe we're going
about it the wrong way.

96 WHO HOLDS THE KEY TO YOUR HAPPINESS?

No one holds the key to your happiness but you.

I know it can seem sometimes that others have the ability to make us feel amazing, or dreadful, but even in those instances there are levels of permissions granted beforehand.

The world doesn't get to determine what makes you smile. If everyone wants to line up for the new iPhone, but you want to run barefoot through the grass with your niece, you can.

We sometimes take the paths that seem to be the right path for us, simply because we see so many others doing the same. When we walk that journey and don't feel the happiness that was advertised to us, we can find ourselves even faking it, or digging ourselves in even deeper.

The reality is if we're not happy with what we have, we won't be happy with what we get. The grass will always seem greener on the other side, because what we really see is a reflection of our envy.

Unhappiness exists when we forget the things we have to appreciate and focus on the things we don't have, or focus on how our realities don't match our fantasies. Fantasies don't end after a certain tax bracket, we'll always want more.

It takes effort to be happy, and to keep it up, but once you find that rhythm, you can share it with others, and spread it like a germ.

The grass will always seem greener on the other side, because what we really see is a reflection of our envy.

97 STARTING IS THE HARDEST PART

We use our imagination to create something we don't want, that's worrying. Worrying leads to fear, fear leads to hesitation and paralysis. Then nothing gets done.

"You don't have to be great to get started, but you have to get started to be great." - Les Brown

I'm most productive when I'm excited. When I finish a track, it feels as if I've laid a final brick on a giant wall, or placed the last stone on a pyramid. I can vibe on the track, and then find energy to start working on another. The most productive element comes from starting. It's the hump that's the hardest to get over, but can fuel momentum to get the job done.

We all feel overwhelmed, the best way to escape that problem is to solve it, head on. Just imagine yourself slowly chipping away. Baby steps in the right direction count, and they'll add up overtime. Patience isn't for waiting; patience is for allowing the necessary time to make things happen.

Right now is a moment you can utilize to move closer to the things that make you happy. It's your life, and you're at the wheel; take it where you want it to go.

"You don't have to be great to get started, but you have to get started to be great."

98 DON'T HOLD YOURSELF BACK

Much of the fear we feel is a result of the ideas we build up in our mind. Our mind knows what we fear, and does a great job using that against us when we try to put it into new and uncomfortable situations.

Discomforting and unfamiliar territories are generally the breeding ground for growth, but that is not a friend to our mind, which prefers remaining in the status quo. For this simple reason, we sabotage ourselves from moving forward.

Positive thinking is simply the practice of encouraging the mind to find all the things that can go right. Our lives are perpetual journeys without a reverse gear. You take a wrong turn, but you're still moving. The longer you turn your head and wallow in that misstep, the farther you'll stray from the path you want to be on.

There really aren't any wrong turns, you are wherever you are. Since that's the only place you're at for the moment, there's nothing to compare it to. If you have clarity of the direction you want to head, you can use that to get back on course, or pave a new road from your current situation.

When we further carve and clarify our chosen purpose on this planet, we'll start to realize when we hit roadblocks that many of them are self-imposed. We give ourselves reasons not to take the leap, and that is a sure sign that we're allowing our fears to get the best of us.

When you want it more than you fear it, you'll get it.

When you want it more than you care about the opinions of others, you'll get it.

When you want it more than life itself, you'll get it.

When you want it that much, there's nothing left to do, but get it.

It's not easy, but with baby steps, you can slowly liberate yourself from the self-imposed prisons we build in our minds. The prisons are layered, and built within each other. With each step, you'll break free of one, only to discover another, that's OK; life wouldn't be much without new challenges. With each step, you'll conquer a fear and acquire a new strength. Take time to reflect and celebrate those triumphs, they'll help you move forward.

When we further carve and clarify our chosen purpose on this planet, we'll start to realize when we hit roadblocks that many of them are self-imposed.

99 HAPPINESS IS NOT A PLACE

Happyville only exists in your head, and it's populated by whatever and whoever you allow in it.

You decide if your mind is full of regret, memories of the past, worries of the future, and toxic individuals who do nothing more than suck the life out of you.

You decide if your mind is full of gratitude, excuses to smile and reasons to enjoy the only moment that matters, the present. You can focus on the people that show you love, or the ones that don't validate you the way you wish they would.

Sh*t's going to happen, some in your favour, others not. How you handle that determines your level of happiness, not the event itself.

Don't get me wrong, I'm in no way, shape or form a Zen Buddha baby, who's constantly at peace with the imbalances of existence. I get just as upset as the next guy, but what I TRY (note the emphasis on TRY) to do is keep it where it needs to be, and not allow it to affect my overall mind state for too long. I also don't promote venting to others. Write your thoughts down, crumple the paper, throw it away, and move on. Other people have their own sh*t to deal with.

At this point if you say my words are easier said than done, you owe me another $5. It's supposed to be difficult; nothing worthwhile is easy, that's what makes it worthwhile.

You can do something simple as writing down things that make you happy. That could be anything from the smile of a cute girl, to your favourite flavour of ice cream. Focusing on happy things helps populate your mind with happy things.

Always be careful of toxic people. You know who's best for you, and who's not. Don't let fear of losing someone stop you from being happy.

"For you to grow, they have to go, so what you stopping them for?"

When you scratch the details, we're all going through the same sh*t, I'd love to hear what you do to populate your mind with happiness. Writing this helped to put a smile on my face.

Sh*t's going to happen, some in your favour, others not. How you handle that determines your level of happiness, not the event itself.

100 SOME FOLKS ARE ADDICTED TO MISERY

Not because they enjoy being miserable, but because they fear the unfamiliar territory that comes with trying to escape it.

If you do the same sh*t everyday you're going to see the same results. If you want a different situation, you're going to have to do something new to make it happen.

Writer Robin Sharma wisely said, "Don't tell me your priorities, just show me your schedule, I'll figure out your priorities from that." If being happy is your priority, it'll show in your daily activities, otherwise it's not important enough in your life.

Actions always speak louder than words.

If our words aren't followed by action then we're just lying to ourselves. Maybe we're even doing it to sabotage ourselves so we can stay in our familiar space, regardless of how miserable it is.

If you want the power to make yourself happy, you have to assume the responsibility for your happiness. Taking responsibility means you can't play the blame game anymore. Once you assume that power, you can break the cycle.

If you want the power to make
yourself happy, you have to
assume the responsibility
for your happiness.

101 THE MOST IMPORTANT CHAPTER IN THIS BOOK

The words in this book have no meaning until they connect with the reader. As an author, I've made peace that once the words go out into the universe, they take a meaning of their own, unique to those individuals who read them.

It's time to write your chapter, this will be the most important chapter in this book. Your reflection of the ideas, and how they relate to your own life is one of the most important ways to reinforce anything and everything you gained from this journey.

I would love to read your chapter, you can send me a copy
feel free to also include all those $5 bills you owe me

Kanwer Singh
6-6150 Highway 7
Suite 226
Woodbridge, Ont
L4H 0R6
Canada

_____
_____
_____
_____
_____
_____
_____
_____
_____

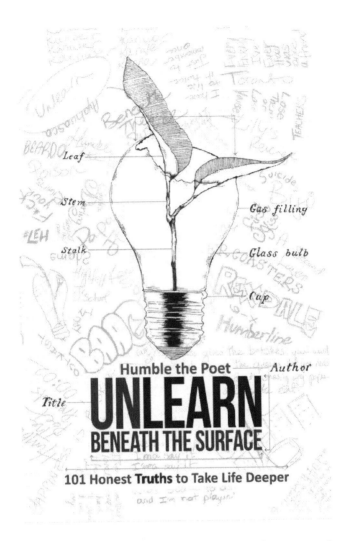

Humble the Poet — *Author*

Title **UNLEARN**
BENEATH THE SURFACE

101 Honest Truths to Take Life Deeper

Beneath The Surface is not a sequel, but rather a second layer to *UnLearn*. It's the next natural step for anyone wanting to take their journey of self awareness and discovery to new depths.

Available at HumbleThePoet.com & Amazon

66267635R00178